ROMANIAN POINT LACE

ROMANIAN POINT LACE

Angela Thompson & Kathleen Waller

B T BATSFORD

First published 2003

© Angela Thompson and Kathleen Waller 2003

The right of Angela Thompson and Kathleen Waller to be identified as Authors of this work has been asserted by them in accordance with the Copyright, Designs and Patents Act 1988.

Volume © B T Batsford Ltd

ISBN 0 7134 8832 8

A CIP catalogue record for this book is available from the British Library.

Printed in China by South Sea International
for the publishers
B T Batsford
64 Brewery Road
London N7 9NT
England

www.batsford .com

A member of **Chrysalis** Books plc

Distributed in the United States and Canada by Sterling Publishing Co., 387 Park Avenue South, New York, NY 10016, U.S.

Book Credits

George Butters Lace supplied for photography from his Romanian lace collection

Bob Challinor Photography on pages 2, 15, 90, 91, 119, 126, 142, and 143

Angela Thompson Historical research, main text, diagrams and samplers; patterns in design section, and photography, apart from those photographs taken by Bob Challinor

Kathleen Waller Instructions for the crochet braids and Christmas ornaments, buttonhole rings, the Celtic set, place mats, coasters and paperweight; also original designs and worked examples for circle sampler, and simple patterns and Ideas for the festive season

Mark Holt Book design

Acknowledgements

Firstly, my thanks are due to all those friends and students who have helped me to discover and improve methods for teaching and working Romanian point lace. Thanks are also due to lace friends who have supplied ideas and information, especially all those Arachne On-Line Lace members who have given support both in England and the United States, to Miriam Gidron for lace books from Israel, and to Landi Phillips for historical facts about Egypt.

I would also like to thank my son, Timothy Thompson, for advice on computer technology and photography; Clive Haines, for tuition in digital imagery; Bob Challinor, for taking the special photographs; and Kenneth Barham, for the use of antique furniture and room settings.

I would also like to thank George Butters, without whom this book would not have been possible, and my friend Pauline Milnes, for accompanying me on our 'Romanian adventure'. My gratitude is also offered to the Romanian family, friends and lace-makers who gave so willingly of their knowledge and hospitality.

Angela Thompson 2002

Obviously without the help of all the above this book would never have been written, but I wish to add my personal thanks to my sister, Margaret Hamer, for checking through my instructions for the braids, the bells and the leaf and the making-up of the place mats.

Kathleen Waller 2002

PAGE 1, FIGURE 1: Circular mat in Romanian point lace (GEORGE BUTTERS COLLECTION)
PAGE2, FIGURE 2: Cushion cover in Romanian point lace, designed and made by Kathleen Waller (PHOTOGRAPHY BY BOB CHALLINOR)

CONTENTS

INTRODUCTION
ROMANIAN POINT LACE
– A JOURNEY OF DISCOVERY

We all have preconceived ideas. When I visited the Lace Group in Romania during 1997 I expected to find a rural village, with the lace-workers sitting in their cottage doorways, making the best of the afternoon sunshine. The reality was entirely different. The original lace co-operative had been set up in the Communist era, but with few sales outlets the women had lost heart. It was not until George Butters, who had originally gone out to Romania to help the orphanages, decided to encourage the workers and bring their lace to England, that the group was re-formed. The lace patterns were divided among the women, most of whom lived in flats in the high-rise buildings that were typical of the Ceausescu era. Other family members and children shared the work, and the lace was assembled later, ready for finishing, washing and stiffening.

The first time I saw this lace was in Hungary in 1993, but it was not until the following year that I was able to purchase a piece from a market stall in Prague, Czech Republic. My lace friend Pauline found an old Coats leaflet that gave instructions for the braid, and later we discovered filling stitches in

FIGURE 3: Lace for sale outside one of the painted monasteries in the central mountain area of Romania

back copies of *Anna Burda* magazines. I was intrigued and wanted to know more.

Through the Arachne On-line Lace Group I was able to contact George Butters, who arranged for Pauline and me to go to Romania and stay with a family in a village in the central mountain area. We combined this visit with a tour of the museums, churches and painted monasteries of Romania. This gave us a broader picture of the country and its craftwork; in fact we saw tapestry-woven carpets and stalls awash with drifts of lace outside every single monastery.

In the Romanian village, the English-speaking daughter, her mother and her grandmother made us very welcome. Florentina was a delightful old lady, with a great interest in needlework of all kinds. The family had invited the lace group to come and meet us. The following day, nineteen members crowded into the small room, each one bringing food for the party – little cakes, biscuits and orange squash. They were happy to demonstrate their techniques and I was especially pleased to learn how to make the little bullion knot grapes, a feature of this type of lace. They laughed at my attempts. In England we hold our crochet hooks and thread in a different way, and I found that this made the grapes awkward to work.

The school children helped to make the crochet braid, a time-consuming process. Some of the workers sewed down the outlines, while others were expert in making the fillings. Later, Pauline and I were invited into the lacemakers' flats. On the outside the tower blocks were dilapidated and worn, with uninviting concrete stairways, but the flats were nicely furnished inside and Romanian lace mats decorated every surface, including the television sets.

I shall never forget the kindness shown to us by the Romanian family and by the lace workers. This has inspired me to learn how to make the lace, as well as to teach, lecture and help to sell the lace. I would like to thank them all, especially Florentina, who, through a translator, told us about the history of the Romanian point lace.

FIGURE 4: The early 17th-century church of the Three Hierarchs at Iaşi in north-eastern Romania is famous for the carved stonework 'lace' patterns on the exterior walls. The carvings, at one time outlined with gold paint, echo the embroidered motifs on Moldavian folk costume

CHAPTER 1

BACKGROUND AND HISTORY

DEFINITIONS AND USES

The lace commonly known as Romanian point is found in many parts of Europe, including Belgium, the Czech Republic, Germany, Hungary and the countries of former Yugoslavia, and also in Egypt and Israel. The English Lace Guild lists the lace as Hungarian point in their collection catalogue. The name Romanian point has been adopted in the United States because Silvia Murariu, who is of Romanian descent, has popularized the lace by privately publishing paperback books on the subject, while Ioana Bodrojan's Romanian point lace is featured in *Piecework* magazine.

The original Coats booklet, *Doilies in Coats Mercer-Crochet No. 525*, published in the late 1960s, gives a pattern for a 'Braid Lace' mat with instructions for making the crochet braid. *Anna Burda* magazine published a series of articles entitled 'Macramé Crochet Lace' during the 1980s. Clearly, there is confusion over the names. The Romanian Lace Group imports a strong cotton macramé thread from Turkey to make their lace. The crochet braid has a slight resemblance to macramé, which has a knotted structure. During the early 20th century, the term 'macramé crochet' was given to a heavy thread lace similar to Irish crochet. The hem edges of this lace were decorated with fringing, thus linking the word 'macramé' to the Turkish word *makrama*, meaning fringed towel.

A traditional braid is plaited. The longitudinal threads interlink with one another to give a pliable result to the structure. Bobbin lace workers will be familiar with this effect, which is found when working half-stitch patterns. A tape is a narrow woven band. Sideways weft threads are woven between the layers of the long warp threads to make a firm structure. Tape does not bend to fit a curved pattern; instead, it must be pleated or gathered. Technically, the crochet braid used in the Romanian point lace is not a true braid, being a looped structure. However, it has all the properties of braid, in that it is pliable

and can be turned in either direction. The crochet braid is worked to form little picot loops at either side. These are essential for linking the foundation threads that hold the filling patterns.

In Romanian lace, the crochet braid is sewn to the curved pattern outlines. The spaces in between are filled with either needlelace or needle-weave stitches. The word 'point' means stitch. So 'needlepoint' means needle stitched, whether it refers to lace or embroidery. Needlelace stitches are looped stitches that are worked into each other in different combinations. Needle-weave stitches are woven in and out of foundation threads that are first laced between the pattern outlines.

Romanian point is a firm lace, used in furnishing and for accessories, pictures and decorations. It is a good alternative for people who have difficulty in working the finer needlepoint laces, and once the stitches are learned, this lace is comparatively easy to make.

ROMANIAN AND OTHER TAPE LACES

It is generally accepted that the term 'tape lace', which includes the braid laces, refers to all those laces that have an outline of tape or braid filled in with needlepoint or bobbin-lace stitches. This does not include those bobbin-lace patterns in which the tape is an integral part of the construction, with elements linked by the working thread. In the 17th century, the tapes were woven on a small ribbon-loom, or worked separately with bobbins on the pillow. They could be plain, or decorated by making pattern holes within the structure. Normally, these flat tapes were folded neatly at the corners, but occasionally they were gathered. Both Italian and Flanders laces were worked in this way, either with bobbin-lace fillings or with a rich variety of needlelace fillings.

During the 18th century laces were fine and delicate, following the fashion for ruffles and dress flounces. It was not until the late 19th century revival that the heavier tape laces came into their own once more. The popular ladies' magazines helped to cater for this interest. The patterns were simple to work and manufacturers provided a variety of tapes and braids. Some of these were very decorative, especially the petal braids used for Honiton point and princess lace. The straight tapes were used in angular patterns for Dickel lace, in England, and interlaced designs for Luxeuil, in Europe. A braid that included draw threads inserted into the edges made Battenburg lace easier to construct. The filling stitches varied from the simplest herringbone with occasional woven wheels to the richness of Devon's Branscombe point lace.

The Romanian point lace is in a category of its own. Other tape laces include needlelace stitches, but none feature the needle-weave fillings that are so typical of Romanian point. It is possible that some fillings developed from the decorative seam-work stitches that were used to join together narrow loom widths of hand-woven fabric in order to make up larger items, such as curtains and bed covers. Many of the full peasant shirts and blouses were joined in this way, but none of the costumes displayed in Romanian folk museums in Bucharest, Braşov, Iaşi and Sibiu showed the use of what we now call Romanian point lace. Neither is it shown in any of the costume books, although costumes were occasionally decorated with torchon bobbin lace or with crochet borders.

It would appear that point lace was a later import into Romania. This theory was borne out by Florentina, the Romanian grandmother, who told us that pattern books from France featuring the lace did not arrive before the 1930s, a date similar to that of the patterns shown in the popular *Stitchcraft* magazine, which included instructions for the braid.

A further French connection was mentioned by an Arachne member, whose elderly friend had been taught this type of lace in a French convent school, when a child in Cairo. Yolanda Minutelli, who was born in Alexandria in Egypt to a family of Italian expatriates, remembers crocheting yards of the braid in the early 1930s. She also attended a convent school and at the age of 12 spent the afternoons working embroidery and lace with her older friends, who were making items for their trousseaux. She had been taught the lace, which they called lacet, by a Syrian girl. This type of tape lace may have been introduced to Egypt by convent nuns from Italy or France. An earlier pattern booklet, *I lavori femminili di mana di fata – il pizzo rinascimento* from Italy, featured the lace and the braid, which has long been used by the nuns for their belts or 'cinctures'.

In Egypt, the early Coptic Christians decorated their woven tunics by leaving areas of warp threads unworked, to be filled in with bands of needle-weaving. This tradition spread through the Mediterranean to Turkey and beyond into Eastern Europe, even reaching into Hungary, where today the weaving stitch is a such prominent feature of Halas needlelace. In Romania and other Balkan countries, needle-weaving patterns within the cloth may be the forerunners of the needle-weave stitches used in the lace. Transylvania, which was once part of eastern Hungary, later became western Romania. This is an important link with other European countries, for much of the original Romanian point lace is said to have come from this area.

Pattern books were printed in Romania during the period 1960 to 1998, while those used by the Romanian Lace Group were dated between1970 and 1976. Today, Romanian point lace flourishes in the United States, popularized by Sylvia Murariu, who was born in western Romania. More recently, Romanian emigrés have taken the lace to Israel and several instruction books in Hebrew have been produced. The *Anna Burda* magazine articles are evidence of a later 20th-century revival in Germany and Central Europe.

Fashions in craft work come and go. It is probable that the lace we call Romanian point developed from the late 19th-century tape laces that were still popular in the 1920s and 1930s. Hopefully, the recent revival will help carry on the tradition.

FIGURE 5: *Patterns carved in the stonework of the 'Lace Church' in Iaşi, Moldavia, north-eastern Romania*

FIGURE 6: *Filling stitches worked on a late 19th-century Branscombe point collar (ANGELA THOMPSON COLLECTION)*

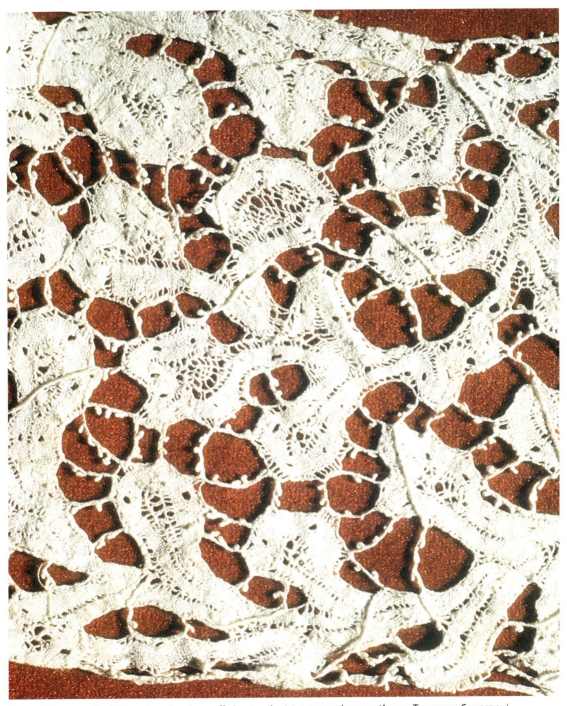

FIGURE 7: *Reverse of a 17th-century Flanders cuff, showing the joins across the tape (ANGELA THOMPSON COLLECTION)*

CHAPTER 2

BASICS

THE BASIC CROCHET BRAID

After working the foundation loops, it is essential to turn the work on the completion of each row. Always turn the same way and work down into the left-hand side loops made on the previous row.

When working the lace fillings, the little picot loops that form on both sides of the braid are used to give support to the stitches.

WORKING THE FOUNDATION BRAID (BRAID 1)

Start with 2 chain (diagram 1a).
In the first chain (1b) work a dc (sc) (diagram 1c).

Turn clockwise.
Work one dc (sc) in the shaded loop (diagram 1d).
Turn clockwise.
Draw the thread through the two shaded loops (1e) and complete the double (single) crochet (diagram 1f).
Note the position of the two shaded loops (diagram 1g).
Turn clockwise.
* Work one dc (sc) through the shaded loops (1h).
Turn clockwise.*

Repeat from * to * until the required length has been worked.

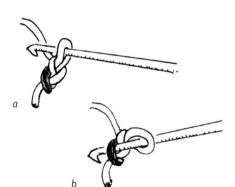

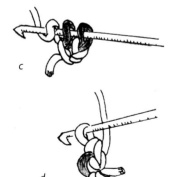

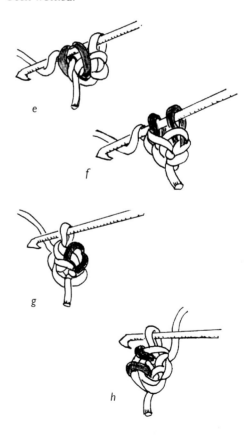

DIAGRAM 1: Stages in working the foundation braid

NEEDLEWORK TOOLS AND MATERIALS

The tools for making the Romanian point lace are simple – tapestry needles to suit the thickness and type of filling thread and a crochet hook to make the foundation braid. A one-piece crochet hook can be used, but the Romanians prefer a hook that fits into a separate handle. This protects the finely-pointed hook, while the cylindrical case serves as a guide to wrap the threads around when forming rings or the thread foundation for the crochet 'grapes'.

A basic knowledge of crochet stitches will enable the worker to produce the foundation braid. Workers with some experience will find the decorative braids and small items well within their capabilities. Beginners with no crochet experience are advised to consult the crochet books recommended on page 140.

NEEDLES

Tapestry needles, which have blunt points, are essential for working the fillings. A pointed needle would catch when needle-weaving or making the needle-looped stitches. Use a no. 24 or 26 for no. 20 crochet thread. Sewing needles are needed for basting the braid to the pattern outline, and a few berry-headed pins are required to keep the braid in place. Small sewing scissors with sharp points are essential for cutting stray ends, and if it is possible to use a thimble, do so. The braid can be quite tough and it may be difficult to push the needle through.

HOOKS

Throughout this book a 1.00mm hook has been used with a no. 20 thread. Adjustments should be made if the braid appears very rigid or very loose. For a finer thread, such as no. 60, a 0.75mm hook is recommended.

HOOK SIZES

Metric	0.75mm	1.00mm	1.25mm
American	13	11–12	9–10

ABBREVIATIONS

	British	American
chain	ch	ch
slip stitch	sl st	sl st
double crochet	dc	(single crochet) sc
treble	tr	(double crochet) dc

NOTE: For all patterns, American abbreviations are given in parentheses.

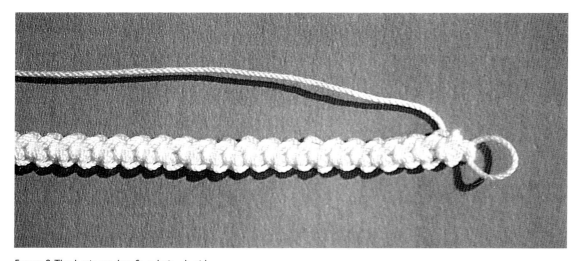

FIGURE 8: The basic crochet foundation braid

THREADS

The weight and thickness of the chosen thread will determine the size of the finished braid. As long as the fillings are in scale with the braid, the thread may be heavy or fine. The one essential is to use a thread with a good, firm twist. Light and fluffy cotton threads, often used for embroidery or knitting, do not give a crisp finish. The Romanians in the lace group used a highly twisted cotton 'macramé' thread, imported at some cost from Turkey. Any make of crochet thread is suitable for both the braid and the fillings, including Turkish threads. For a list of stockists, see page 141.

CROCHET THREADS

Coats Anchor Crochet no. 20 works well for normal use, no. 40 and no. 60 for finer work, and a no.10 for coarser work. Coats Opera no. 20 has a slight sheen. These threads come in a range of plain and shaded colours.

DMC Cordonnet Spécial no. 20 or no. 10 may also be used. Alternatively, use the range of threads called Fils à Dentelles. For finer work use nos. 40, 50 or 60.

Flora produce a variety of threads, including a no. 20 mercerized thread in 100 per cent cotton, made in Bulgaria, while a no.10 thread for coarser work is made in Japan by YLI.

Turkish thread comes in plain and shaded colours. A no. 50 is equivalent to a crochet no. 20. Altin Basak Klasic no. 50 has been used for some of the examples in this book.

METALLIC THREADS

Several types of metallic thread, produced for embroidery as well as for crochet, are suitable either for making the braids or for working decorative effects within the fillings.

Güttermann produce a range of threads called Metallisiert. These are intended for embroidery, but are useful as highlights within the fillings. YLI Candlelight comes in shaded colours, including gold and silver. These metallic threads, made in Japan, can be used for crochet braids as well as for the decorative fillings.

Madeira has a series of metallic embroidery threads, which can be used for the fillings.

JOINING THE BRAID THREAD

If possible, try to make the correct length of braid for the project, plus a little extra to allow for unravelling. Occasionally, the thread may run out or it may be necessary to continue a part-completed braid. To join threads in 'mid-stream', leave 30cm (12 in) of the last working thread. Pick up a new working thread; tension this around the fingers, and work the next crochet stitches with the new thread. After a few rows have been worked, pull the two loose threads in opposite directions, thread each end with a needle and work one up and one down into the foundation braid. Cut off the ends.

FIGURE 9: Threads for Romanian point lace; the cards in the background designed and worked by Kathleen Waller (PHOTOGRAPHY BY BOB CHALLINOR)

STARTING – PREPARING THE PATTERN OUTLINE

As in all other needlepoint laces, Romanian point lace is supported on a backing fabric while it is being worked. The pattern is traced on the backing; the braid is basted to the pattern outline, and the filling stitches are worked in the appropriate spaces left between. The braids are joined where they touch. Brides, or bars, with the optional inclusion of buttonhole rings, are used to connect wider spaces. When all is finished, the basting stitches are removed to free the completed lace. The pattern can be used again.

METHOD 1

The Romanian Lace Group was short of materials. They used old sheeting for the backing fabric, drawing out the pattern with a ballpoint pen and covering all with a sheet of thin plastic, basted down at intervals. For this method, use a cotton or similar fabric in white or a pastel shade.

Trace the pattern onto the fabric, using a fibre-tipped pen. The use of a light box or piece of glass illuminated from below is recommended. Either place transparent plastic on top of the fabric, or use thin, coloured plastic bags to provide a contrast. Baste out from the centre in both directions and at intervals to hold in place. Architect's linen, if available, is an alternative backing. This is a pale-blue transparent fabric-film, with a slight sheen on one side.

METHOD 2

The second method is suitable for smaller projects. Trace the pattern on tracing paper, using a fibre-tipped pen. Alternatively, photocopy the pattern on thin typing paper. Trim to size.

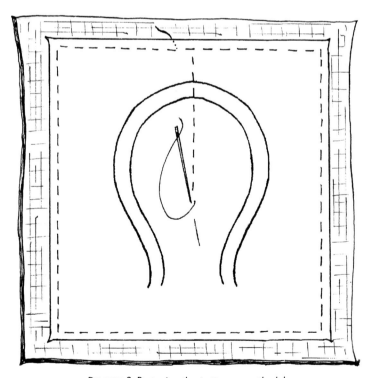

DIAGRAM 2: Preparing the pattern – method 1

Cut a piece of pale-blue sticky-backed film of a similar size. The film is available from lace-makers' suppliers. Peel off the backing and stick the film onto the pattern. Cut a slightly larger piece of non-iron interfacing and baste the pattern to this, basting first all round the edges, and then from top to bottom and side to side. Trim the corners of the pattern and backing to a curve to prevent the working thread from snagging (see the illustrations under Starter Pattern on page 70).

ATTACHING THE BRAID TO THE PATTERN OUTLINE

Measure the required length of braid by laying it roughly around the pattern outline. Allow extra for joining. Simple patterns that have only one join are easier for beginners. To join ends, unravel the braid to give a length of thread long enough to be taken through the crochet loops. Secure these loops and then use the thread to sew the braid ends together. After sewing, the surplus is taken back up through the braid and cut off. It is easy to unravel the braid from the working end, but not quite so easy to unravel from the beginning end.

Using a strong sewing thread in a contrasting colour, sew the braid in position around the pattern outlines with ladderstitch (see diagrams 3a and b). On the right side, parallel stitches cross the braid at intervals; on the wrong side, upright stitches alternate at the sides. Fasten the basting thread to the reverse of the backing fabric; bring the needle up through the fabric, and start by sewing two or three stitches over the braid in the same place. While stitching, ease the braid into position with the fingers, taking care not to push or stretch the braid during the work. Sew corners with a series of fan-shaped basting stitches. Finish at the braid end with two or three stitches in one place, taking the basting thread through to the reverse of the backing fabric. It is important to sew the braid down firmly. When the decorative filling stitches are worked, they can cause the braid to distort and pull out of place.

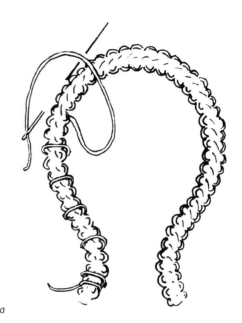

a

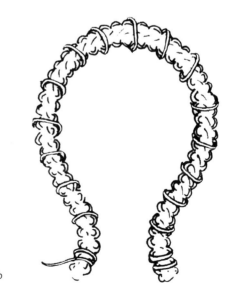

b

DIAGRAM *3 a and b: Stages in attaching the braid to the pattern outline*

CHAPTER 3

FILLINGS FOR OVAL AND SIMILAR SHAPES

VERTICAL FOUNDATION THREADS – FAN-SHAPED

The pliable nature of the crochet braid makes curved shapes easy to achieve. For this reason, many of the traditional Romanian point laces feature flowers with oval petals. The variety of filling stitches gives a richness to the lace, allowing the worker individuality of expression. Needle-weave stitches are worked over a fan-shaped foundation of threads that is sewn through the picot loops that border the inner edges of the crochet braid. These threads can be the same colour as the braid or provide a contrast. Fillings can be worked over an even or uneven number of threads at each side of the central point, depending on the pattern. The stringing threads are usually worked into every other picot loop, but sometimes it is necessary to work the shapes either closer or more spaced out, depending on the pattern and the size of the space to be filled.

HANDY HINT: as a temporary guide for counting, tie a contrasting thread into the picot at centre top of the curve.

METHODS FOR FASTENING ON AND LAYING FOUNDATION THREADS

Start by taking a thread about one metre, or just over a yard, in length. The higher the number of foundation threads, the longer this initial thread needs to be. Fasten on by taking the tapestry needle about halfway down the curve and threading it through as far as the point at which the thread bridge is to be made. Secure with a backstitch. Work across the gap to the opposite side to form a thread bridge, then bring it back to the starting point (diagrams 4a and b).

COUNTING AND STRINGING

Decide on the number of threads per side and count every other picot loop downwards from the centre on the right. Remember the position of this

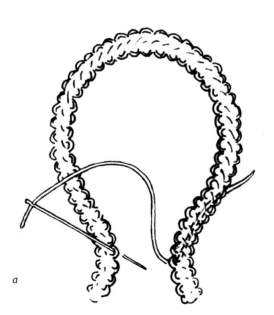

a   *b*

DIAGRAM 4: *Making the thread bridge*

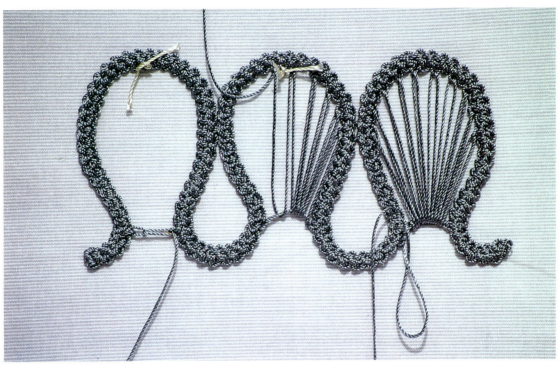

FIGURE 10: Stages in stringing the foundation threads

c

last loop. From the starting point at the right of the foundation bridge, take the thread up to the chosen picot loop, and go down through the loop and back down to the thread bridge (diagram 4c). Come from under the bridge and then go back up into the alternate picot loop above the first one. This is like working a figure-of-eight, threading between the thread bridge and the picot loops.

Continue until all the threads are in position. Fasten off with a backstitch before threading through the braid on the opposite side. Cut off the end. If working from left to right is preferred, reverse the instructions. Unless otherwise stated, these double threads count as one thread when working the needle-weave patterns. Remove the contrasting thread guide.

With practice, counting becomes instinctive.

NEEDLE-WEAVE STITCHES

The names given to the fillings described here and elsewhere are not traditional, but are descriptive terms used for easy identification. The filling names are listed in the Index, page 144.

The length of the weaving thread will be determined by the type of filling.

OBELISK

String up six double threads on each side of the central point.

Cut a length about one metre, or just over a yard. Fasten on at the right side by taking the working thread through the braid and start to weave over and under every two pairs of threads (diagram 5). Continue needle-weaving for 12 rows.

Next row, from the right, work to the two central pairs and continue weaving on these pairs for another 12 rows. Leave out the two outer thread pairs and work up the two remaining pairs. After eight rows, take the needle back down through one of these pairs and cut off the thread end (diagram 6).

HANDY HINT: if the working thread proves to be too long for any particular filling, take note of the length and adjust for any similar fillings.

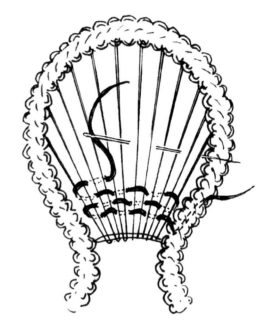

DIAGRAM 5: Weaving over and under double threads

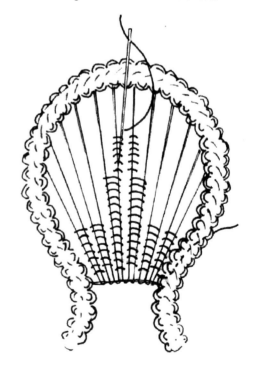

DIAGRAM 6: Taking the needle back through the finished work

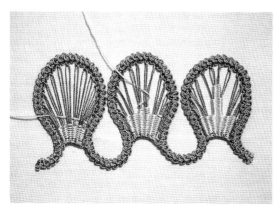

FIGURE 11: Obelisk

ZIGGURAT

String up either eight double threads on each side of the central point, or a number divisible by four.

Fasten on at the right side and needle-weave over and under every four sets of double threads for eight rows. Then weave over the two right-hand pairs only for six rows. Leave out the right pair and pick up the next left pair. Work these for six rows. Repeat. Weave up the four remaining central pairs and at the top take the needle back down, as shown in fig. 12. Work back down, reversing the instructions. Take the final thread down through the original foundation weave. Finish by taking the thread through the braid on the left-hand side, and cut off the end.

HANDY HINT: do not work the top pairs too tightly or it will be impossible to take the needle back through.

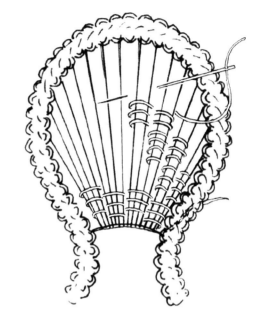

DIAGRAM 7: Working the right-hand side

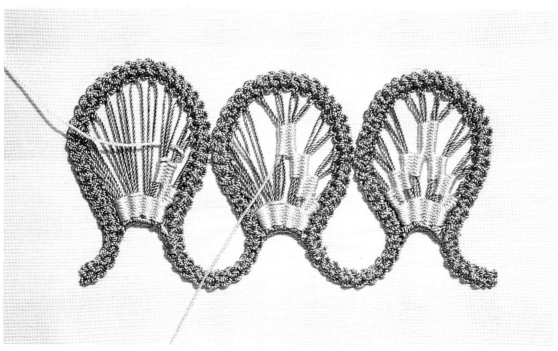

FIGURE 12: Ziggurat

ARABESQUE

For this combination of needle-weaving and needle-wrapping, string up five double threads on each side of the central point.

Fasten on at the right-hand side. Start by wrapping the working thread four times around all the foundation threads so that they are drawn together evenly. Next wrap around the first three right-hand pairs only, six times. Leave out the left-hand pair and wrap over the two remaining pairs six times. Leave out the left-hand pair and wrap one pair only. Take the needle down through to the centre, ready to start weaving the central area. Needle-weave up the two central pairs eight times. Then take in the pairs on each side for six rows. Take in the next two pairs on each side for six rows (diagram 8). Finally leave out two pairs for six rows, twice. At the top take the needle down to the centre and work the left-hand side wrapping, in reverse order.

HANDY HINT: check the pattern for mistakes every two rows. Do not try to work back, but un-thread the needle and gently pull out the weaving thread.

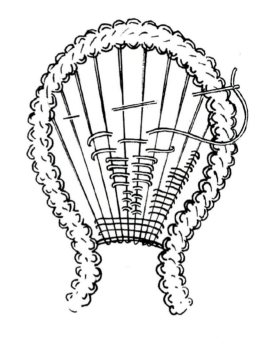

DIAGRAM 8: Weaving the central area

FIGURE 13: Arabesque

FIGURE 14: Divided wheat ear

DIVIDED WHEAT EAR

This needle-weave features a central division. To start, string up six double threads on each side of the central point.

Divide the stringing threads at the centre and needle-weave for six rows, pulling all together tightly but evenly. For the next six rows, work over and then under the right outer pair, over five pairs to the centre, under five pairs and over the left-hand pair. Continue to leave out one pair on each side every six rows until the final centre pair at the top is reached. Work six rows and take the needle back down through the central pairs. Cut off.

PLAIN WHEAT EAR

This is the same as divided wheat ear, but without the central division. Wrap all the threads for four rows, and then continue as before, leaving out pairs on both sides until the final pair at the top. Work six rows and take the needle back down through the central pairs. Cut off.

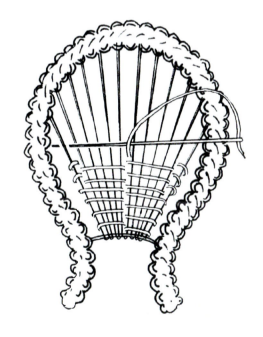

DIAGRAM 9: Weaving with central division

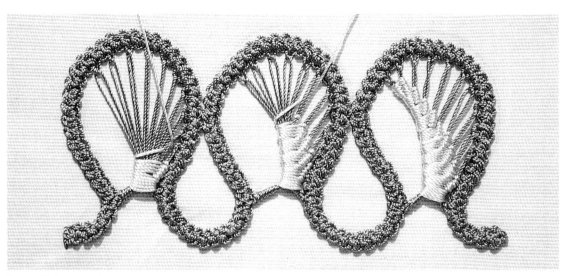

Figure 15: Asymmetric curve

ASYMMETRIC CURVE

Asymmetrical fillings can look very decorative, either on their own or arranged in groups. They can be worked as mirror-image motifs to form a double petal, or they may all face the same way in a circle.

HANDY HINT: use a small hand mirror to judge the effects of mirrored repeats.

String up six double threads to the right of the centre and three double threads to the left. Row numbers can be adjusted to suit the size and shape of the motif.

Starting at the right, wrap round all nine threads six times. From the left, weave six rows, under and over the right-hand pair, then back under the remaining eight pairs. Leave out one right-hand pair every six rows until only two pairs are left at the top. Work a final six rows before threading the needle back down though the wrappings at the left-hand side. This pattern also works with six threads on one side and four on the other.

HANDY HINT: when stringing up, make the thread bridge fairly tight; the tension on this one-sided pattern may cause distortion.

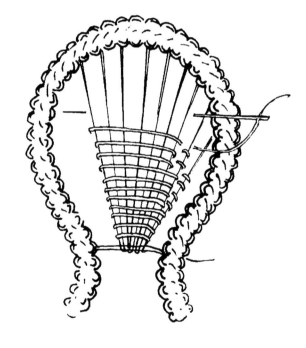

Diagram 10: Weaving method for leaving out the right-hand threads. For pattern row numbers see instructions.

DECORATIVE CURVE

String up five double threads on the left-hand side of the centre and four doubles on the right.

Work in the same way as for the previous filling, but start from the right-hand side. After every five rows of weaving, leave out one double pair at the left-hand side. The curve is determined by the number of rows worked before leaving out a pair. Fewer rows make a shorter curve, more rows a longer curve. This time, room is needed to work the top detail of the pattern. When only two double threads remain, work five rows. Then leave out the double thread to the right and weave four rows by adding in the double to the left. Repeat. Finish at the left on the same level as the last right-hand double thread (see diagram 11).

HANDY HINT: adjust the top weaving with the point of the needle until it sits in a neat curve.

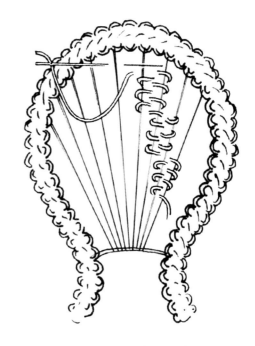

DIAGRAM 11: Working the detail of the top filling

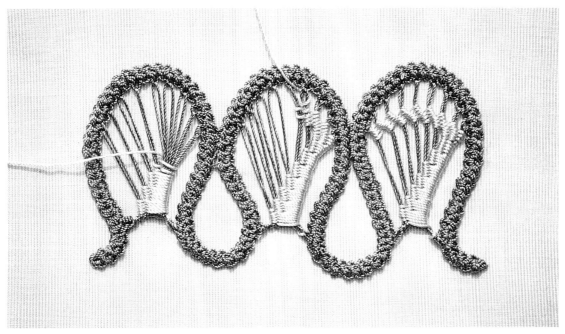

FIGURE 16: Decorative curve

ARCHED CENTRE

For this filling, which features needle-weaving on both sides of the centre, first string-up six double threads on each side of the centre.

Divide the threads in the centre and start working on the right-hand side. Weave in a similar way as for the previous filling, leaving out the right-hand pair of threads after every six rows until only one pair is left. Take in the next pair to the left of centre, weave six rows, thread the needle back though the left-hand side and continue to work downwards, this time taking in the next pair of threads at the left-hand side and weaving six rows. Finish off at the bottom by threading into the braid in the usual way. The number of rows between each pattern change can be altered to suit individual needs, but it is easier to keep to the same number each time, odd or even.

HANDY HINT: keep a count of the rows worked so that each side is of equal size.

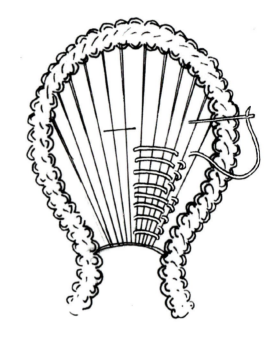

DIAGRAM 12: Working the right-hand side

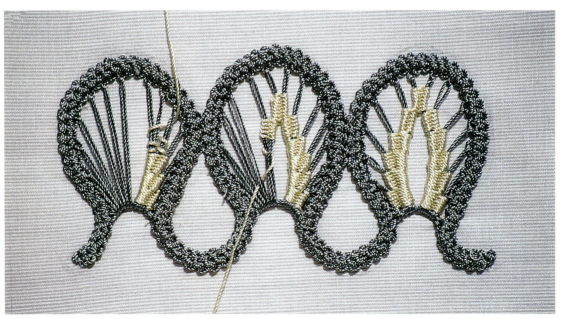

FIGURE 17: Arched centre

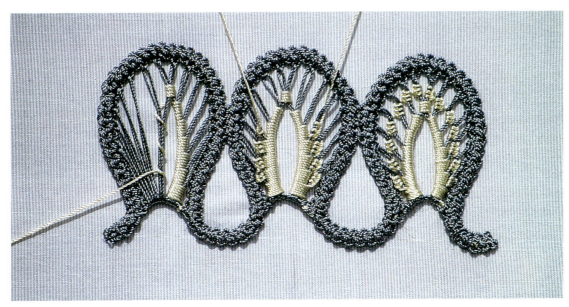

FIGURE 18: Fancy arched centre

FANCY ARCHED CENTRE

This is a combination of needle-wrapping with a buttonhole border. Start by stringing-up seven double threads on each side of the centre.

Divide the threads in the centre and start working on the right-hand side. Wrap the seven double threads evenly for six rows. Leave out one double thread at the right and wrap the remaining six double threads for six rows. Repeat until only one double centre thread is left at the top. Wrap this together with the next pair on the left, four times. Take the needle down, ready to work in reverse, taking in a double thread at the left after every six rows. Fasten off.

The buttonhole-stitch borders are worked from the bottom upwards with two separate threads. Secure within the braid at each side and work three buttonhole stitches over each double thread in turn. Come up from underneath the double threads at the start of each buttonhole set (see diagram 13). Finish off at the top by taking each thread end down through the needle-weaving to the bottom. Trim off.

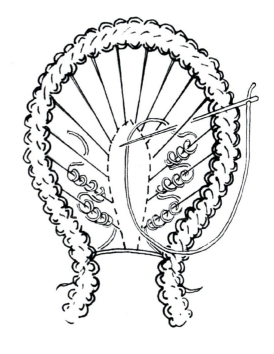

DIAGRAM 13: Working the decorative border

BRANCHED TOP

This needle-weave filling has a divided, or branched, top. First, string up five double threads on each side of the centre.

Divide the threads in half and needle-weave under and over ten double threads for five rows. Drop the two outer double threads and weave for five rows. Continue to drop the outer threads on each side every five rows until only the two central double threads remain. Weave for five rows. Working on the right-hand side, weave in and out of each of the five double threads for four rows.

Leave the outer thread unworked and weave for another four rows. Repeat until two double threads remain to the right of the centre. Weave four rows, take the needle back down through to the centre and repeat the weaving pattern in reverse. Take the thread down through to the centre on the left side and cut off.

> **HANDY HINT:** if the thread runs out, take the end out through the braid at the side, re-thread the needle and enter at the same place. Alternatively, hide the threads within the needle-weaving.

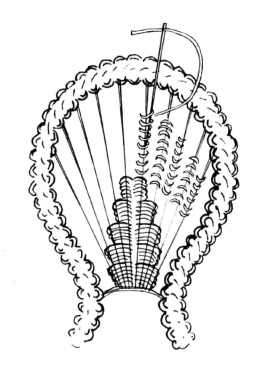

DIAGRAM 14: Taking the needle back to the centre

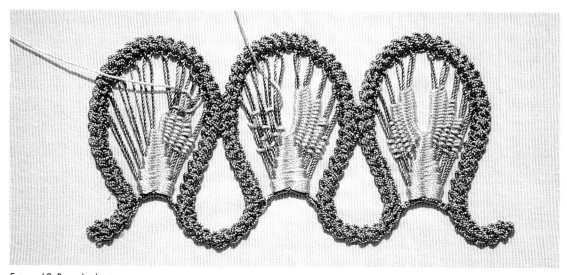

FIGURE 19: Branched top

PYRAMID BASKET

String up eight double threads on each side of the centre.

Choose four, five or six thread rows in a block to suit the oval shape. Starting at the bottom right, needle-weave over all 16 double threads as described below.

First set of five rows – work over seven, under one, over one, under seven double threads.

Second set of five rows – work over six, under two, over two, under six double threads.

Third set of five rows – work over five, under two, over two, under two, over five double threads.

Fourth set of five rows – work over two and under two double threads across the row.

Fifth set of five-thread blocks – leave out a double thread on either side and repeat every five rows until only two blocks of four are left. Finish off by working over and under the two central double threads and take the needle back through the work as usual.

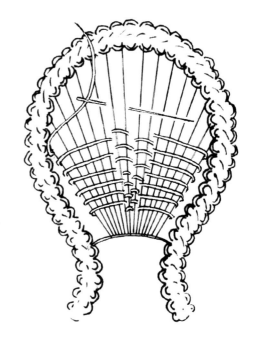

DIAGRAM 15: Weaving the first two sets of thread blocks. For pattern numbers, see instructions

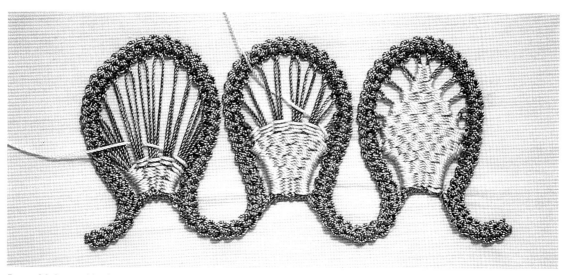

FIGURE 20: Pyramid basket

ZIGZAG BUTTONHOLE BORDER

String up six double threads on each side of the centre.

Needle-weave six rows over and under every two pairs of double threads. Thread back down through the right-hand side and come back up through the braid a short distance above the completed needle-weaving.

Work four looped buttonhole stitches up the first two double threads on the right. Split these two thread pairs at the top, leaving out the first pair and picking up the next pair to the left. Work four buttonhole stitches down these two pairs of threads. Split the threads again, leaving out one pair and taking in the next one (diagram 16). Work up and down in this manner until the left-hand braid is reached. Fasten off within the braid.

DIAGRAM 16: Working the buttonhole zigzag

FIGURE 21: Zigzag border

FIGURE 22: Plaited basket

PLAITED BASKET

String up five double threads on each side of the centre.

Needle-weave seven rows under and over every two pairs of double threads. Work eight rows under and over every single pair of threads. The number of rows worked can be adjusted to accommodate a particular pattern area. Finish on the right-hand side.

To work the plaited top, fasten into the braid on the right-hand side. This is optional, but it helps to keep the plait in place. Work two stem stitches over the first two pairs of threads to the left. Leave out the right-hand pair and take in the next left-hand pair, then work two stem stitches over these two pairs. Continue across the row. Take two stem stitches into the left-hand braid (optional) and then work in reverse, back to the right. The stitches should sit neatly, sharing the same thread intersections.

HANDY HINT: do not work the plait too tightly or it will distort the basket top.

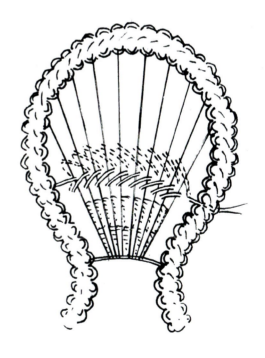

DIAGRAM 17: Working the basket stem-stitch plait

NEEDLE-LOOPED AND NEEDLEPOINT LACE STITCHES

Traditional needlelace is composed of a variety of needle-looped stitches that are worked into each other to form a lace structure. Although these looped stitches are not true buttonhole stitches, they are frequently referred to as such. In accordance with common usage, the term 'buttonhole stitch' is used here in this context.

CENTRE LINKS

For this filling of grouped needle loops, fasten on the working thread at the bottom right-hand side. Take the thread across into the opposite left picot loop, then back to the start. Repeat twice more, going into the next two immediate picots above the first. From the bottom right, wrap the thread over the first thread group and into the first picot above to the right. Repeat twice more into the next two picots above. Wrap the thread around the previous thread group, and work to the left once more. Repeat, alternating the thread groups until all the picots are filled on both sides. Fasten off at the top within the braid. The number of threads in each thread group is optional as long as the same number is used each time.

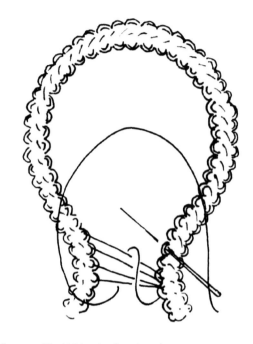

DIAGRAM 18a: Linking the first thread group

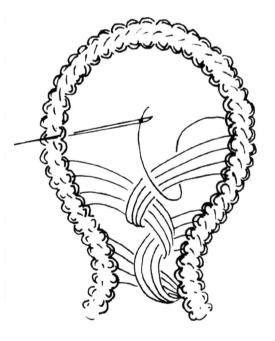

DIAGRAM 18b: Starting the fifth thread group

FIGURE 23: Centre links

HERRINGBONE LATTICE

This is a combination of buttonhole bars with herringbone in-fill. Four double thread bars are sewn across the braid loop motif at intervals. Start at the bottom right-hand side and make the foundation bridge as usual. Thread up inside the right-hand braid and come out above. Make a double bar across and then cover with close buttonhole stitch. Coming up through the braid, make two more buttonhole-covered bars, spaced evenly. Starting at the top left-hand side, work figure-of-eight herringbone stitches into the picots above and buttonhole loops below. Thread into the braid, right-hand side, and work the row below back to the left by going into the buttonhole loops both above and below. For the bottom row, work the herringbone over the foundation bar, finishing at the buttonhole bar above, then through the braid at the side.

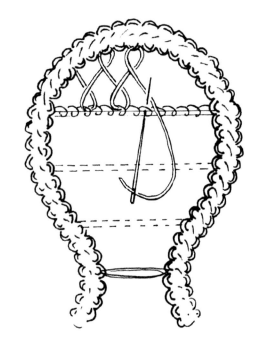

DIAGRAM 19: Herringbone stitch filling

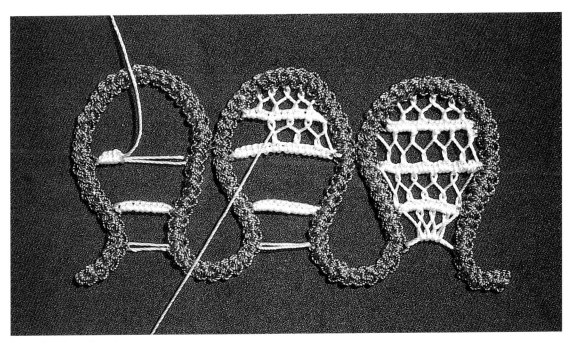

FIGURE 24: Herringbone lattice

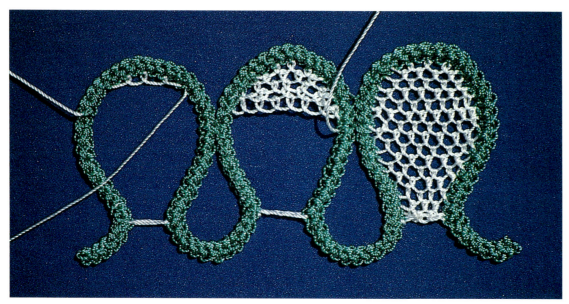

FIGURE 25: Single Brussels stitch

SINGLE BRUSSELS STITCH

This needle-looped filling is one of the classic needlelace stitches. It is one of the simplest but not necessarily the easiest to do as it is essential to maintain an even tension throughout the work. A foundation row of buttonhole-loop stitches is worked first, then on every subsequent row the stitches are worked into the row above, thus forming a network of lace stitches. It is not until the final anchoring row that the work attains stability.

Starting at the top left of the braid oval, make buttonhole-loop stitches into every other picot, with the central loop worked into the top central picot. Work into the braid at the right-hand side, ready to come back with a second row of loops, each worked into the loop formed above. Working backwards and forwards, increase the number of loops as the oval shape widens then decrease as it narrows. Finish by working the final row into the bar at the bottom.

HANDY HINT: many needlelace stitches can be used as Romanian lace fillings (see the book list on page 140).

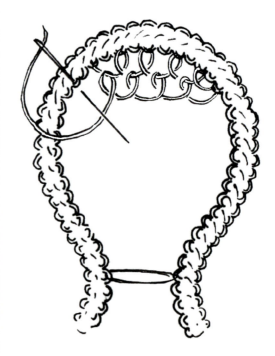

DIAGRAM 20: Working the first two stitch rows

NEEDLELACE TRIANGLES

The same Brussels needlelace stitch is used for this needlelace filling, but this time it is spaced into groups.

Make a bridge across the bottom as usual. For even results, it is necessary to count out the picots available. On the sample, three groups of seven picots were worked, with four left empty between, each time. Starting at the bottom right, leave four picots, work a loop into each of the next seven picots, leave four picots and repeat until four empty picots remain at the bottom left. Go over the foundation bar and work back up the left-hand side, this time working only five loops into the six above. Leave a bar across the gap and work five loops into the top six loops. Repeat, going over the bottom bar at the right-hand side, then working back up again. On each row, the number of loops diminishes by one for each group, finally leaving only one loop on each triangle. Loop the three together, come back to the bottom bar and needle-weave the threads together for five rows before finishing off by going back through and into the braid.

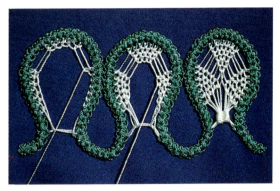

FIGURE 26: Needlelace triangles

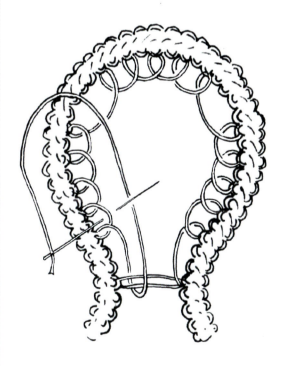

DIAGRAM 21a: Starting the loops, working into five picots

DIAGRAM 21b: Beginning the second row of loops

CHAPTER 4
FILLINGS FOR LONG, NARROW AND LEAF SHAPES

———— ✿ ————

Narrow shapes need particular stringing methods to hold the filling stitches. The picots at the side of the braid can be linked with a ladder of thread bars worked into every loop or into alternate loops. A herringbone stitch foundation gives a more open construction. Buttonhole and feather stitches, worked in various combinations over the thread bars, make decorative fillings. Further variations using mirror images of the stitches add a richness to the repertoire.

THE SUPPORT STITCHES

Ladder bars are threaded by fixing into the braid at the base of the shape. Come up through the first picot loop, then take the thread across and down into the loop on the opposite side. Come up into the next loop above and go back across and down into the opposite loop. Repeat to the top of the ladder and finish off in the braid as usual.

MAKING A PRACTICE SAMPLER

A stitch sampler will serve both as a handy reference and as an opportunity to practise. Cut a small piece of single-thread canvas (the kind used for canvas work or needlepoint) of about 12 holes per inch (2.5cm). Cover this with thin iron-on interfacing, allowing extra to turn under, and smooth the rough canvas edges. Use the holes, which are still visible, as guidelines to satin-stitch a ladder of bars up the surface of the canvas. Feather stitches are worked downwards over these thread bars, starting from the top. The stitches do not go through the backing fabric, relying on the thread bars for their support.

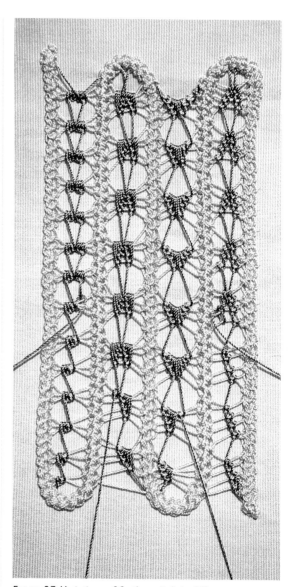

FIGURE 27: Variations of feather stitch in different combinations, some alternating, others mirror-imaged by working downwards from the top with two separate threads.

MAKING A PRACTICE SAMPLER

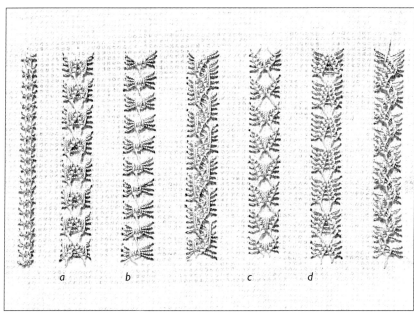

a Feather stitch groups worked over two, three, four and five bars with the second set mirror-imaged

b Buttonhole groups worked over four bars

c The same stitch as in 28a, but with the second set mirror-imaged the opposite way

d Feather stitch groups worked over two bars (see diagram 23)

FIGURE 28: Buttonhole and feather stitch variations worked over ladder bars

DIAGRAM 22: Single feather stitch is worked over three bars, alternating after every fourth stitch.

DIAGRAM 23: Single feather stitch is worked to the right downwards over two bars in groups of four, repeated after missing one thread. A second row is worked similarly, but to the left.

NEEDLE-WEAVE AND TWISTED CHAIN STITCHES

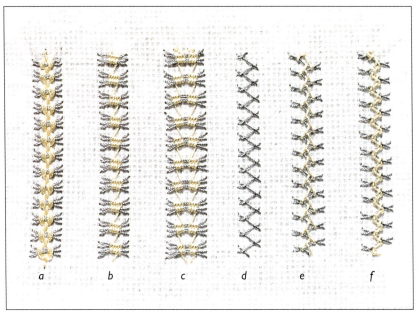

FIGURE 29: Needle-weave stitches on bars, feather and chain stitches on herringbone

a Also illustrated on page 43 (see diagram 34)

b Groups of four needle-weave stitches worked over four bars (see diagram 24)

c Two rows of similar needle-weave stitches worked in mirror image

d Herringbone stitch foundation worked over the canvas

e Feather stitch over herringbone worked the other way up

f Twisted chain worked over each herringbone intersection (see diagram 25)

DIAGRAM 24: Blocks of needle-weave stitches are taken over four bar-threads. Miss two threads and repeat

DIAGRAM 25: Twisted chain stitch is worked over the triangle points of herringbone foundation

ZIGZAG FILLING STITCHES

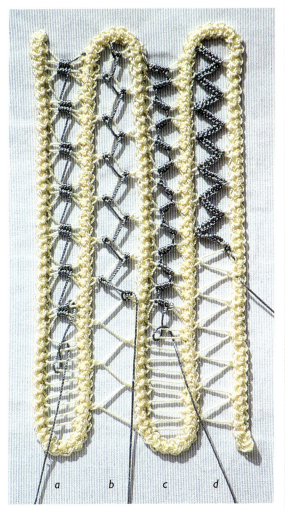

FIGURE 30: Needle-weave and buttonhole stitches worked over bars and herringbone lacing

a Needle-weave stitch is worked over groups of four bars.
b A double buttonhole stitch is worked over every spaced herringbone foundation.
c Six close buttonhole stitches cover two bars, alternating from side to side.
d Zigzag foundation bars are laid by missing two picots and working into one, both ways. Cover with close buttonhole stitches.

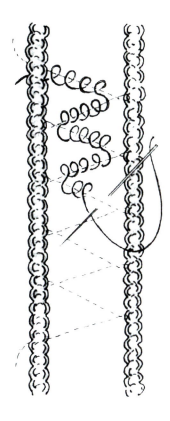

DIAGRAM 26a: Buttonhole stitch is worked over a herringbone foundation

DIAGRAM 26b: Detail of the buttonhole loops over the foundation thread

DECORATIVE FILLINGS

The following fillings are more complicated than those on the previous pages, but are well worth trying out. Make another covered-canvas sampler before attempting the patterns on the lace motifs.

Both 31a and 31e are worked over the usual thread ladder bars and are variations of closely worked alternating feather stitches. To work these fillings, follow diagrams 27 and 28. A plaited effect will appear in the middle.

Examples 31b and 31d are woven across two vertical foundation threads, linking into the braid loops on either side (follow diagrams 29 and 30).

The example shown in 31c has a central needle-woven bar worked over two vertical foundation threads. During the stitch construction, thread bars are worked into the braid loops at either side, and then buttonhole stitched over on the return journey (follow diagram 31).

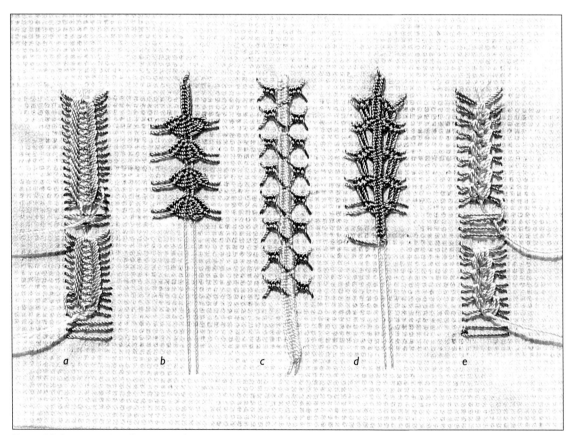

FIGURE 31: Five examples of decorative fillings

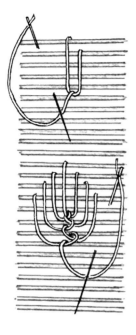

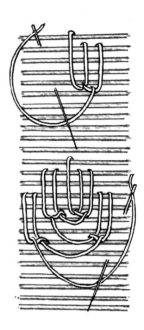

Diagram 27: Plaited feather stitch, single

Diagram 28: Plaited feather stitch, double

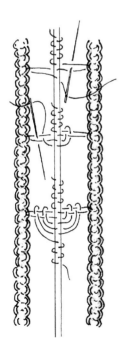

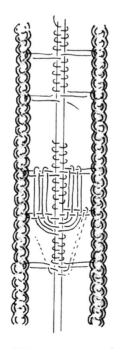

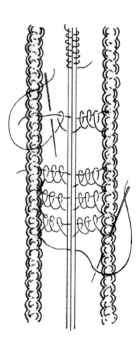

Diagram 29: Decorative weave 1

Diagram 30: Decorative weave 2

Diagram 31: Buttonhole cross filling

FILLINGS FOR LEAF SHAPES

Any of the stitches listed in the previous section are suitable for narrow leaf shapes. The motifs are strung across with ladder bars or herringbone lacing linked into the braid loops.

In fig. 32a and c, herringbone lacing supports alternating double feather stitch (see also diagrams 32a and b). Herringbone lacing is used as a filling stitch in figure 32b, being worked into every picot loop. Fig. 32d and e show chain stitch worked over ladder bars (see diagram 33). In 32f, chain stitches are combined with a double herringbone centre.

A vertical double support thread is first laid behind the ladder bars. It can be the same colour as the bars or contrast with them. Fasten on at the top and at the bottom of the leaf motif.

In fig. 33a a double support thread is laid behind the ladder bars. In 33b and c, the working thread is interwoven round the bars and double thread (see diagram 34). For 33d, a single support thread is laid behind the ladder bars, while 33 e and f show the working thread woven in circles round the bars and support thread (see diagram 35).

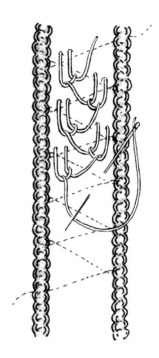

DIAGRAM 32a: Double feather stitch on herringbone laced foundation

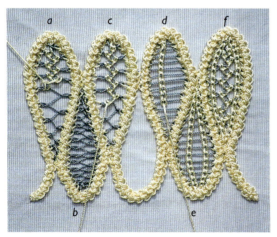

FIGURE 32: Feather and chain stitches on herringbone lacing and ladder bars

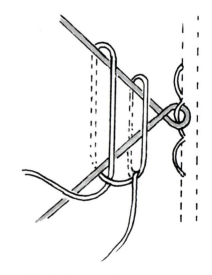

DIAGRAM 32b: Feather stitch detail

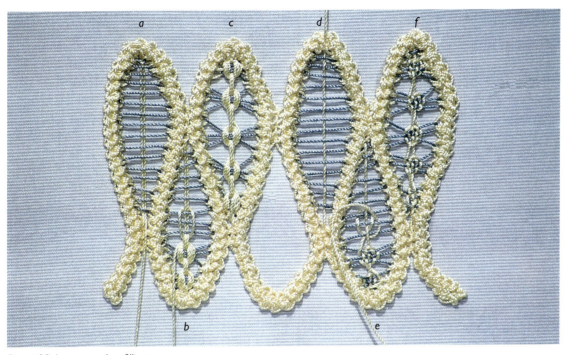

FIGURE 33: Interwoven bar fillings

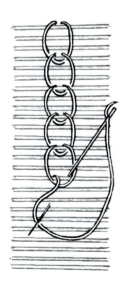

DIAGRAM 33: Chain stitch worked on ladder bars

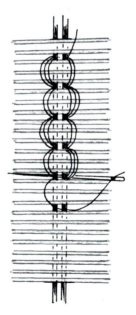

DIAGRAM 34: Interweave on a double support thread

DIAGRAM 35: Circular interweave on a single support thread

FILLING STITCHES WORKED OVER HERRINGBONE LACING

FIGURE 34

a Herringbone is laced into every third picot loop. Groups of four buttonhole stitches are worked on alternate herringbone intersections.

b Herringbone is laced into every fifth picot loop. A second set of herringbone lacing is worked evenly spaced between the first set. Buttonhole loops (single Brussels stitch) are worked into the resulting lozenge shapes. Take in the foundation threads at the sides and base of the lozenge (see diagram 36).

c Circular weaving around a foundation of double herringbone lacing (see diagram 37).

d Needle-weave triangles on single herringbone lacing: the needle is taken back through each right-hand triangle, ready to start the next one on the left (see diagram 38).

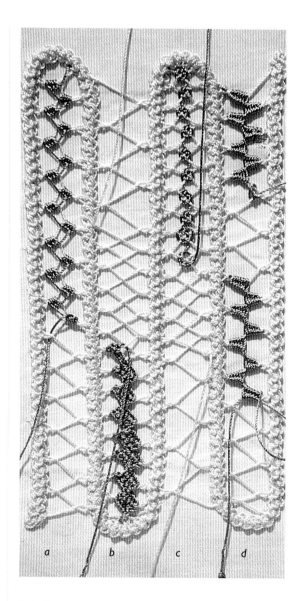

HANDY HINT: always go down into the picot loop when lacing herringbone stitch. The needle comes up from below the thread, ready to cross over on top to the opposite loop.

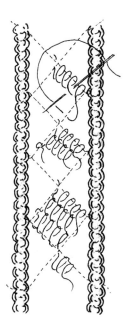

DIAGRAM 36: Buttonhole loops worked over double herringbone lacing

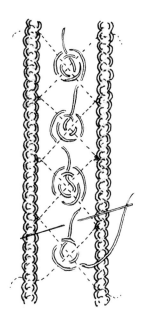

DIAGRAM 37: Circular weaving worked round double herringbone lacing

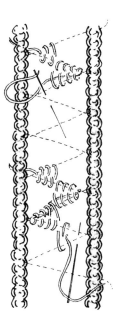

DIAGRAM 38: Needle-weave triangles worked on double herringbone lacing

CHAPTER 5

FILLINGS FOR SMALL ROUND SHAPES

NEEDLE-LOOPED AND NEEDLE-WEAVE FILLINGS

Circular fillings can be based either on needlepoint lace patterns or on woven and spider wheels. Many are derived from embroidery techniques or from the traditional designs worked over cloth-covered buttons. Needle-looped fillings are worked into the picot loops on the inner circumference of the circle, every other one, or every third one, according to the pattern.

Wheel and spider-web patterns require a foundation of looped wheel spokes, which are worked at regular intervals diametrically across the circle into the picot loops of the braid. Fasten the working thread into the braid and stitch across to a picot on the opposite side. Come back to the centre, link in the middle with the first thread and continue across to the next chosen picot loop. Return to the centre and continue until the required number of double-thread spokes is in place. Finish in the centre to start the pattern.

> **HANDY HINT:** for even spacing, count the picot loops and divide by the number of spokes.

WINDMILL SAILS

Work an uneven number of loops into the braid circle. On subsequent rounds, work the new loop stitch into the right of the one above. On each round, the working stitch takes in all of the loops formed above. This will give a staggered effect of woven triangles (see fig. 35a).

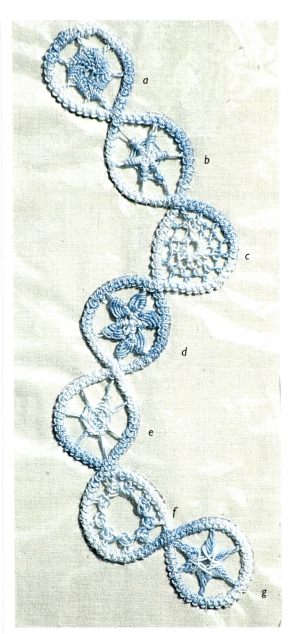

FIGURE 35: Needle-weave and needle-looped circle fillings

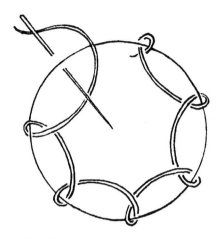

DIAGRAM 39a: Working the foundation loops

BACKSTITCH WHEEL

Choose an even number of wheel foundation spokes and finish in the centre. Starting at the centre, work backstitch around the spokes by taking the needle under two spokes, then back over one spoke. Continue until the wheel is partially filled. Finish off by taking the thread through the back of the work, or back out to the braid circle (see fig. 35b).

STEM STITCH WHEEL (see fig. 35e)

This pattern is stem-stitched from the top by taking the needle over two spokes, then back under one spoke.

DIAGRAM 39b: Working the second round of loops

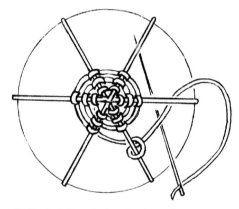

DIAGRAM 40: Backstitch worked under the spokes

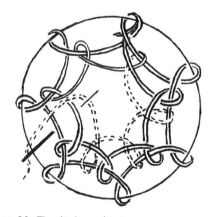

DIAGRAM 39c: The third round in progress

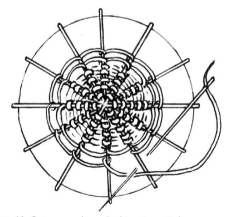

DIAGRAM 41: Outer rounds worked in stem stitch

BRUSSELS LACE CIRCLE

A series of single loops is stitched into every other picot of the inner braid circle. On the second round, each new loop is worked into the one above, as in single Brussels stitch. There will be one less stitch on each round until the centre is reached. Draw up the remaining few loops and secure with a stitch, or work back through to the outer circle braid (see fig. 35c).

PETAL WEAVE

Lay an even number of spokes. Start at the centre and work three or four rounds of backstitch to secure the threads. Taking the first two spokes, weave in and out of both legs, gradually increasing the width of the stitch. Make sure to finish under the second spoke before continuing to work over the next spoke. This spoke shares the set of woven stitches just completed, together with those of the next petal set. Ease the stitches so that they lie flat (see fig. 35d).

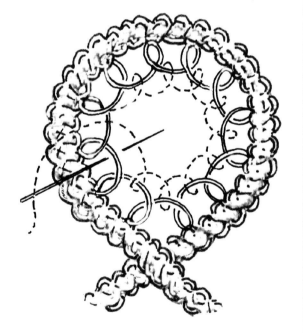

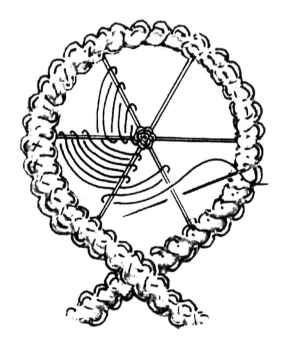

DIAGRAM 42: First and second rounds of the needle-loop stitch   *DIAGRAM 43: Needle-weaving the petal shapes*

ROSE RING

Work eight loops into the circle, keeping the tension fairly loose. Next, using the working thread, stitch in and out of the base of the loops, as shown in diagram 44a, to make a firm foundation ring. Continue with the same thread, or chose a different colour for the roses. Weave in and out of both the loops and the foundation thread in a pattern of double circles (see fig. 35f).

STAR LOOPS

Needle loops are stitched into the outer braid with even spacing. The second row of loops is worked under the crossing of the initial loops of the first round. The needle does not go through the loop, but behind it. Each subsequent round is worked in the same way, so that the loops build up around the first one, eventually filling the centre of the circle. Finish off by taking the thread back through the stitches. Take care to see that each loop sits outside the corresponding one on the previous round (see fig. 35g).

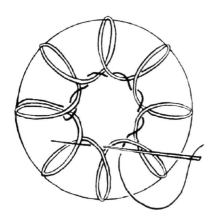

DIAGRAM 44a: Working the foundation ring

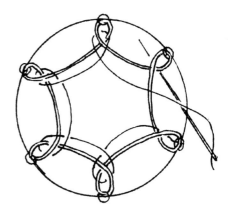

DIAGRAM 45a: First and second loop rounds

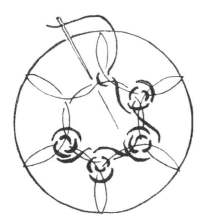

DIAGRAM 44b: Weaving the rose circles

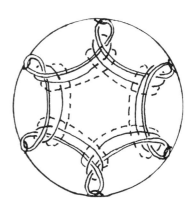

DIAGRAM 45b: Third and subsequent loop rounds

HOW THE FILLING PATTERNS ARE USED

Not all braid outlines are completely round, oval or a simple leaf-shape. Flower petals are often indented at the top or heart-shaped. Ovals can be elongated, while leaf shapes may be pointed at both ends or at the base only. Shapes can curve and change direction, or alter in width. The lace-worker needs to be flexible in adapting the various fillings so that they fit the shapes without distortion and do not look crowded or too spaced out. The following flower-petal shapes show the use of various fillings illustrated in the previous chapters.

FIGURE 36: Flower in shaded thread

Starting from centre top, clockwise:
  Single Brussels lace filling
  Fancy arched centre
  Feather stitch on herringbone lacing
  Plaited basket
  Herringbone lattice
  Decorative curve
The centre is filled with a backstitch wheel and petal weave.

FIGURE 37: Three-heart blue flower

Starting from centre top, clockwise:
  Interwoven bars
  Decorative curve
  Obelisk, worked twice
The centre is filled with a backstitch wheel.

The patterns for these flowers, which are designed and worked by Kathleen Waller, can be found on page 101 (see diagrams 68 and 69).

FIGURE 38: First pink and cream flower

Starting from right top, clockwise:
    Fancy arched centre
    Decorative curve
    Ziggurat
    Branched top
    Wheat ear
    Arched centre
The centre is filled with backstitch wheel.

FIGURE 39: Second pink and cream flower

Starting from centre top, clockwise:
    Buttonhole zigzag
    Double-feather stitch on herringbone lacing
    Single feather- and chain-stitch rows
    Stem-stitch groups and buttonhole filling
    Needle-weave filling
    Needle-weave filling with centre chain
In the centre, wrapped bars support a buttonhole-stitch-covered hexagon.

CHAPTER 6
DECORATIVE ADDITIONS

RINGS

Small rings, applied on top of or included as part of the Romanian point lace, add both interest and a focal point to the overall design. They can be made in a needlelace technique and covered with buttonhole stitch or, if preferred, worked as a ring in double (American single) crochet.

BUTTONHOLE-COVERED RINGS

First mark four lines on graph paper, drawing them at right angles to each other, the ends nearest to the central point being equidistant from it. Cover the paper with architect's linen (see p.16) or a similar transparent sheet and baste in place. Make four basting stitches on the marked lines.

To make the ring, using the chosen thread, work the needle under the basting stitches for two or three rounds (more if a heavier ring is needed).

Buttonhole-stitch around this foundation, cutting off the tail when firmly secured. On completion, leave a length of thread ready for use and detach the ring from the backing sheet. To make a larger ring, mark off six lines as shown and work in a similar way.

CROCHET-COVERED RING

Wind the chosen thread about six times around a pencil or crochet hook handle, according to the size required. Slip the ring off the pencil, taking care not to disturb the thread rings, and work double (single) crochet into the thread ring to cover completely. For a thicker ring, work two or three rounds of double (single) crochet on top of the first. This is the foundation for the crochet version of the bullion knot grapes described on page 57.

> **HANDY HINT:** crochet or buttonhole rings may be worked over a plastic or metal ring used as a former.

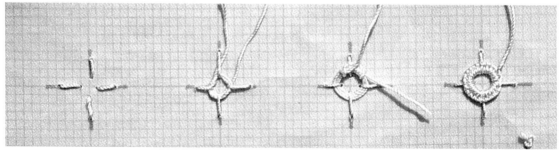

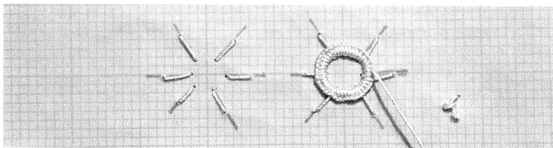

FIGURE 40: Making buttonhole rings on foundation threads

Using the ring stick for predetermined ring sizes

Ring sticks may come in pairs, one larger than the other, to give a choice of diminishing sizes for ring-making. They are cylindrical in shape, with a series of steps turned into the wood, each one smaller than the last, tapering towards the top with every step.

The thread is wound several times around the chosen circumference. The wound thread holds the starting thread in place. When the ring is thick enough, thread the working end into a needle and, holding the thread rings carefully, slip them a short way up the ring stick. As the circumference narrows, the rings will loosen slightly. This allows the needle to be passed under all the threads at once, ready to work the first buttonhole stitch. In order not to distort the thread ring, pull the thread into position carefully and continue to work buttonhole stitches around the ring. The tail end of the starting thread will be covered by the buttonhole stitches. When it is firmly held, cut off the tail. After one round, the thread ring may be pushed off the ring stick and a second round worked on top if necessary.

Make the buttonhole ring with the thread that is to be used for the fillings. The finished ring is sewn onto the lace, in the chosen position. The rings look best when placed at a junction where braids join, or at some focal point within the design. Make them the same colour as the lace, or to contrast. Alternatively, these buttonhole rings can be incorporated with the joining bars that hold areas of the braid outline. This makes an attractive background for the design motifs.

Handy hint: always leave a tail of thread long enough either to be used to sew the ring in place onto the lace or to make at least one of the joining bars within the pattern.

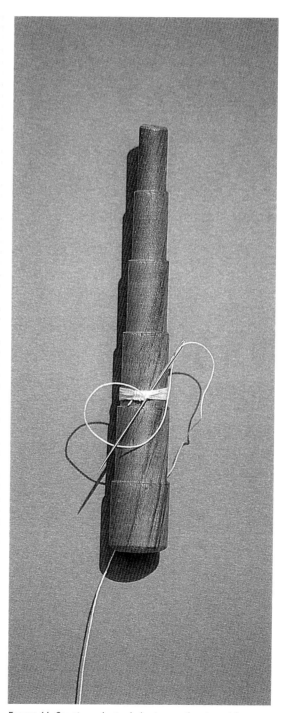

FIGURE 41: Starting a buttonhole ring on the ring stick

BULLION KNOT GRAPES

Grapes can be applied to lace, either at intersections or in the centre of a flower. A favourite motif is the 'bunch of grapes'. A triangular motif is formed of the individual grapes, joined together at the sides through the crochet loops, and then attached to a stalk with leaves.

FIGURE 42: Different types of bullion knot grape:

Right – grape-and-leaf motif made by the Lace Group expert

Top centre – grape-and-leaf motif from western Romania

Left – grape-and-leaf motif from Israel

Bottom centre – single grapes (top left from central Romania and, underneath, two grapes by the Lace Group expert)

FIGURE 43: Detail of grape motif lace displayed on a car, central Romania

FIGURE 44: Detail of the grape motif shown in top centre of fig. 42

The three-dimensional circular motifs known as bullion knot grapes are one of the distinctive features of Romanian point lace. Many of the pieces of lace for sale outside the Romanian painted monasteries or on wayside stalls feature grapes within the designs. In a resort town in the central mountain area, the lace was displayed on the windscreens and tops of parked cars. One handsome lace mat, decorated with clusters of the grape motifs, stood out from the others. The grapes are neatly worked and formed with a shallow dome, but the bullion knots do not completely cover the padding (see fig. 43 on page 55 for detail).

As my collection of Romanian lace began to grow, it became apparent that there were variations in the shape of the bullion knot grapes. These differences were not ones of technique – each grape being worked with bullion knots laid over a core of threads – but rather of the structural shape. The variations appeared to correspond to different geographical locations, rather than to any preference by the individual worker.

Some of my earlier lace mats were purchased from a Women's Institute tutor who had visited Romania for a folk dance festival. The grapes on these mats are similar in size and shape, but much firmer. Two lace mats came as gifts from Israel. The first, bought in Jerusalem, had grapes worked with a very loose tension over a soft inner padding. Although attractive, they lack the crispness of the other grapes. The assumption that this was a characteristic of the Israeli lace proved to be wrong, for a second gift from an Israeli pen friend contained well-made grapes, high-domed and with a hard centre.

Even better grapes were made by the Romanian Lace Group. One member worked quickly and accurately to produce superb examples. This was her speciality and she did nothing else. The grapes are not easy to make, as the crochet hook is used to pull a loop through 20 twists of thread. The Romanians hold the crochet hook from the top and this may give more control to the tension.

WORKING THE BULLION KNOT GRAPES – NEEDLE METHOD

The crochet method is not easy for beginners, so try a needle-stitched version first.

Begin by winding the working thread 20 times round a pencil or ring-stick. Slip the thread circle off the 'former' and work about 20 buttonhole stitches into the thread ring.

DIAGRAM 46a: Placing the needle through the ring, ready to start the bullion knot

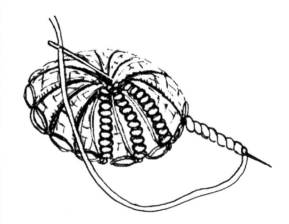

DIAGRAM 46b: Winding the working thread around the needle end before taking the thread through

Work around again on top until the required amount of padding is reached. *Bring the thread up through the ring, ready to put the needle back down through the centre of the ring (see diagram 46a). Wind the thread 20 times around the protruding needle end and pull the thread through, making a bullion knot* (see diagram 46b).

Repeat from * to * until 15 to 20 bullion knots are spaced evenly around the thread ring (see diagram 47 for finished results).

CROCHET HOOK METHOD

First wind the thread 20 times around a pencil or the base of a crochet hook. Slip the thread circle off the 'former' and work about 20 dc (sc) into the thread ring. Work a second round of dc (sc) into the thread ring, on top of the first round. For a larger grape, work a third round of dc (sc) into the ring.

*Put the hook down through the centre of the ring and wind the thread 20 times around the hook (see diagram 48a). Draw a loop of the working thread through the wound thread, easing it gently. Do not make the windings too tight or it will be impossible to get the loop through. With the loop still on the hook, put the hook down through the centre of the ring and make a dc (sc) * (see diagram 48b). This enables the bullion knot to stay in place with one strand of thread (part of the double [single] crochet) lying to one side. Continue by starting the second knot.

Repeat from * to * and make from 15 to 20 bullion knots before finishing off (see diagram 47 for finished results).

DIAGRAM 47: The finished grape, showing bullion knots in position

DIAGRAM 48a: Wind the thread around the crochet hook end, ready to pull the loop through

DIAGRAM 48b: Work a double (single) crochet stitch to secure the bullion knot in place

JOINING BARS

A type of lace consisting of separate motifs joined together by a series of bars with spaces in between is called a guipure lace. There are no fillings worked within the ground – the name given to the background of the lace – whether this is needle-weave, needlelace or bobbin lace. In some laces, these bars are called 'brides' or 'legs'. Whatever the name, the function is the same – they serve as a decorative element in the design and hold the lace together when it is removed from the pattern support. The bars can be worked at regular intervals or placed by the worker at random, giving a 'crazy-paving' effect.

In bobbin laces, these bars, or brides, are worked as plaits, sometimes single, sometimes double, but within a needlelace, the bars are formed of thread 'bridges' which are then covered with a thread wrapping or with buttonhole stitch.

FIGURE 45: Romanian point lace showing the use of joining bars within the pattern
(ROMANIAN LACE FROM THE COLLECTION OF GEORGE BUTTERS)

The guipure technique is an effective method for joining separate braid-outlined motifs in Romanian point lace. In some pattern drawings, the bars are indicated, but in others the placement is left to the discretion of the worker. It is essential to work out beforehand where the bars are to be included. A random placement can lead to overcrowding in some areas, while in others the lack of bars will make the finished lace unstable. Draw out the pattern outlines with a waterproof fibre-tipped pen, and then add the bars in pencil. These pencil lines can be rubbed out if they look wrong, then inked in when corrected. It is perfectly acceptable for a group of bars to come together in a point at one end to make a fan-shaped arrangement.

Sometimes a buttonhole ring is held suspended within the design by a series of bars radiating out into a circle shape.

FIGURE 46: Detail of Romanian point lace showing the use of joining bars and woven wheels within the pattern (ROMANIAN LACE FROM THE COLLECTION OF GEORGE BUTTERS)

MAKING THE BARS

Do not attempt to include any of the joining bars
until all the braid-outlined motifs are completed,
along with their chosen fillings. The filling stitches
tend to pull and distort the outlines of the lace.
Even the experienced worker finds that the finished
lace will 'shrink' when removed from the pattern
support, as the braid is no longer held at tension.
This is a feature common to all laces, not only
Romanian point, and it is thus essential that the
braid outlines be ladder-stitched firmly in place to
reduce this problem.

MAKING A WHIPPED BAR

This is the simplest form of bar. Fasten on the
working thread by taking the needle through the
braid as usual, then coming out at the starting place
for the bar. Take the thread across to the picot on
the braid at the opposite side of the gap. Come back
to the starting point and go through the braid picot
loop. Work back again to the opposite side, so that
there are three threads forming the foundation of
the bar (see diagram 49, top section).

Cover the bar by wrapping the working thread over
and around the foundation bar until it is
completely covered. Try to keep a constant tension
so that the threads lie evenly. If necessary, it is
possible to arrange the wrapped threads with the
point of the needle afterwards, but it is better to
make them lie correctly in the first place. Finish off
by taking the thread through the braid at the side.

MAKING A BRANCHED BAR

Work the three foundation threads for the bar as
before. Whip the bar to half way, and then work a
branched foundation out to the opposite side of the
gap by linking into the braid outline at a point
some short distance away. Whip the branched bar
back from this outer point until the part-completed
bar is reached. Join on here and complete the
whipping of the bar. Finish off by taking the thread
through the braid at the side (see diagram 49,
bottom section).

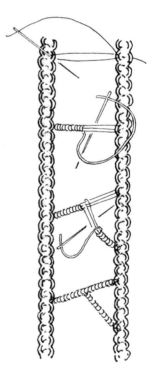

DIAGRAM 49: The stages in making a whipped bar, together
with branched bars

ADDING PICOTS TO THE WHIPPED BARS

Lay the thread foundation bridge as before and whip halfway across the bar. Place the needle behind the unwrapped foundation threads and, taking the working thread between finger and thumb, wind the thread twice around the needle point. Pull the needle through the loops to form the picot, easing the knot up and into place. This is similar to making a French knot in embroidery, but with an extra turn. Complete the whipping of the bar (see diagram 50).

MAKING A BUTTONHOLE-COVERED BAR

Lay the three foundation threads for the bar as before. Work back over these threads with close buttonhole stitches to cover the bar neatly. Try to work them all at one time, so that the bar does not twist over, causing the stitches to kink in the middle (see diagram 51, top).

ADDING PICOTS TO A BUTTONHOLE-COVERED BAR

Work halfway across the bar. Hold a loop of the thread in place, either with a pin or with the fingers. Take the thread over the bar and form a second loop. Place the needle behind the first loop and the pin, then through the second loop. Pull the thread into place carefully, so as not to distort the picot (see diagram 51a).

MAKING A BULLION KNOT PICOT

Work halfway across the buttonhole bar. Place the needle down into the bar of the buttonhole stitch that you have just completed. Wind the thread at least seven times around the needle. Pull the thread into place carefully, thus forming a bullion knot. Continue to buttonhole stitch over the foundation thread bar. The bullion knot picot will form into a little loop. The more twists on the knot, the bigger the loop. In some needlelace versions, the knot is made by taking the needle into the upright of the last buttonhole stitch made, rather than into the bar of the previously worked buttonhole stitch (see diagram 51b).

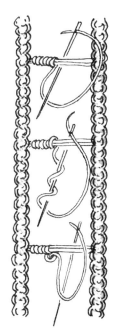

DIAGRAM 50: Stages in making a picot on a whipped bar

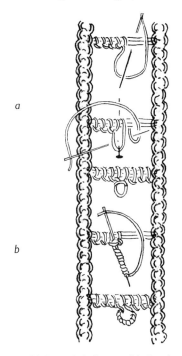

a

b

DIAGRAM 51: Buttonhole loop and bullion knot picots on buttonhole bars

CHAPTER 7
BRAIDS

While the narrow basic crochet-braid (Braid 1 – see page 12) is excellent for outlining the majority of pattern motifs, decorative braids add richness and variety to the lace, whether used as an outline or as an integral part of the design.

The Romanian lace workers use these decorative braids to great advantage. They are fond of asymmetric patterns and use wide braids to make sweeping arcs through the lace, reminiscent of certain Art Nouveau designs. The peoples of the Balkans and Eastern Europe have a different way of looking at pattern, possibly influenced in the past by the Turks, who brought ideas from the Middle East. It is worth studying the use of braids in Romanian lace. There is much that we in the West could learn from these examples.

One advantage of the use of braid within the lace is that it is a speedy way of filling the pattern area. It could be argued that the fancy braids take time to make, but their construction is less involved than the more detailed working of the lace. For those with some knowledge of crochet, the braids are not difficult to make, and they add a new dimension to the lace work.

Braids can outline certain areas on the borders of the lace, form part of the internal structure of the lace, or be used to make fillings inside a narrow braid outline held at each side with a pattern of herringbone lacing.

Worked in glitter threads, braids can be used to make Christmas decorations. A series of braids, worked in several colours, make an unusual but effective greetings card when held within a card mount. This is a way of using up odd pieces of leftover braid; alternatively, longer lengths can be worked, then cut to size as required.

ILLUSTRATIONS OF BRAID USE
For other uses of the braid, see page 84, and also the Christmas tree decorations on page 91. For inclusion of braid within the lace, see the Romanian lace angel on page 103, which features three of the braids in order to suggest pattern and texture. Braids form an integral part of the design for the tea-cosy illustrated on page 107, and the butterfly designs on pages 110 and 114 are both outlined with one of the braids, chosen to give a more delicate edging than the firmer basic braid.

Further examples of braids forming an integral part of the design can be found in the Gallery of Traditional Romanian Point Lace, starting on page 128.

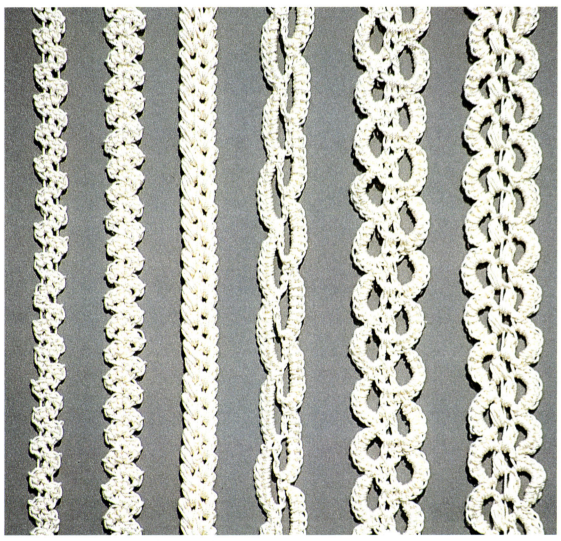

FIGURE 47: Decorative crochet braids numbers 2–7

DECORATIVE BRAIDS

For abbreviations and hook and thread sizes, please refer to pages 13–14.

BRAID 2

Start with two chain, three double (single) crochet into first chain made. One chain, turn.

One dc (sc) into first dc (sc). Two dc (sc) into front of the loop of the second dc (sc). One chain, turn.

Repeat from * to * until the required length has been worked.

BRAID 3

Start with three chain. One dc (sc) into the middle chain, and three dc (sc) into the first chain. One chain, turn.

One dc (sc) into the first dc (sc), three dc (sc) into the next dc (sc). One chain, turn.

Repeat from * to * until the required length has been worked.

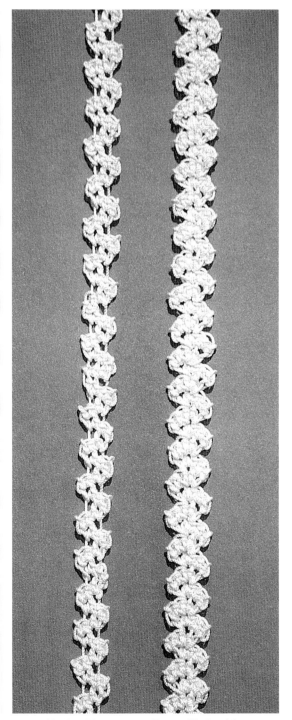

FIGURE 48a: Braid 2   FIGURE 48b: Braid 3

BRAID 4

Start with three chain. Draw the yarn through the first chain (two loops on hook).

Yarn around the hook, draw the yarn through the first chain (four loops on hook)

Yarn around the hook and draw the yarn through the first chain again (six loops on hook).

Draw the yarn through the six loops, one chain to bind them together, thus forming a cluster.

One chain, turn.

Make a cluster into the same place as the first. One chain, turn.

In the last cluster but one, make a cluster, inserting the hook so as to leave a pair of threads to the right of hook, one at the front and one at the back of the work. One chain, turn.

Repeat from * to * until the required length has been worked.

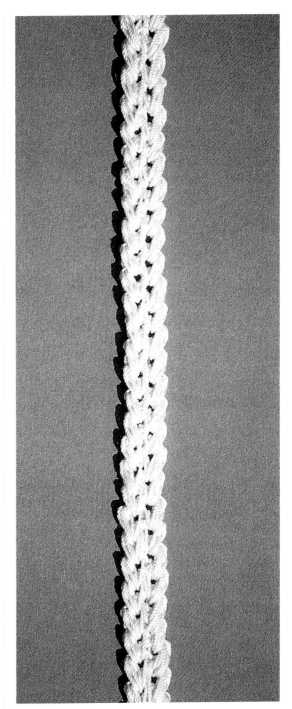

FIGURE *49: Braid 4*

BRAID 5

Start with nine chain, sl st into the first chain.

Turn, nine dc (sc) into the chain loop.

Nine chain, sl st into the first chain of the first nine-chain loop.

* Turn. Nine dc (sc) into the chain loop just made.

Nine chain, sl st into the ninth dc (sc) worked in the last loop but one.*

Repeat from * to * until the required length has been worked.

FIGURE 50: Braid 5

BRAID 6

Start with three chain (this counts as one treble [double], one chain). One tr (dc) into the first chain.

Five chain, sl st to the first chain at the base of the treble (double).

Turn, eight dc (sc) into the five-chain loop.

One tr (dc), one chain, one tr (dc) into the space between the first three chain and the treble (double).

Five chain, sl st into the first chain of the starting chain.

Turn, eight dc (sc) into the five-chain loop. One tr (dc), one chain, one tr (dc) into the space between the previous two trebles (doubles). Five chain, sl st to the eighth dc (sc) of the last but one set of eight dc (sc) worked.

Repeat from * to * until the required length has been worked.

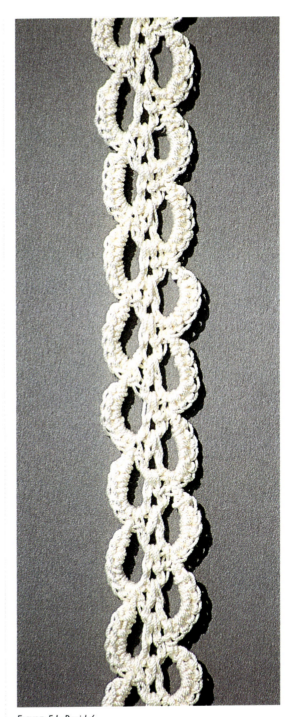

FIGURE 51: Braid 6

BRAID 7

Start with three chain. Draw the yarn through the first chain (two loops on hook).

* Yarn around the hook. Draw yarn through the first chain * (four loops on the hook).

Repeat from * to * (six loops on the hook). Draw the yarn through these six loops, one chain to bind them all together, thus forming a cluster.

Five chain, sl st into the first of the three chain.

Turn, eight dc (sc) into the five-chain loop. Two chain, one cluster into the first three-chain loop.

Five chain, one sl st into the base of the first cluster.

Turn. Eight dc (sc) into five-chain loop. Two chain, one cluster into the two-chain space before the previous cluster. Five chain, one sl st into the eight dc (sc) of the last but one set of eight dc (sc).

Repeat from ** to ** until the required length has been worked.

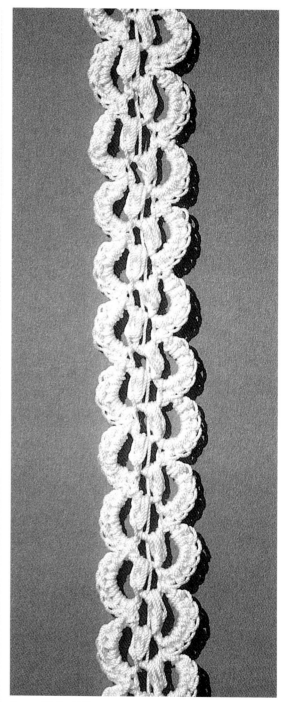

FIGURE 52: Braid 7

CHAPTER 8

SIMPLE PATTERNS

STARTER PATTERN

The filling stitches detailed in the previous sections, together with the methods for making rings, grapes, bars and braids, are intended as a reference for some of the designs available in Romanian point lace. The worker can choose any suitable fillings for this starter pattern, or use the ones illustrated in fig. 56.

The little flower and leaf motif has been chosen as a starter pattern because it contains the basic construction elements found in most types of Romanian point lace. The curved petals are common elements in floral motifs, as are leaf shapes and circles. The leaf shapes have pointed ends, while a curved stalk supports the flower head. The motif is made with one continuous length of braid, so there are only two end joins. In other parts of the design the braids are joined where they touch. The methods included in the working of this pattern can be applied to any of the other Romanian lace designs.

DIAGRAM 52: Starter pattern – flower and leaf motif

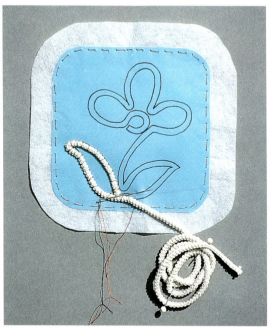

Figure 53: Sewing the braid to the pattern outline using a ladder stitch

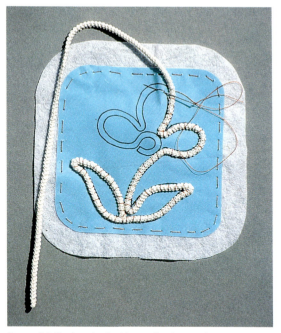

Figure 54: Sewing the braid round points and curves

Figure 55: Laying the foundation threads for the fillings

FIGURE 56: The finished flower motif features fan, leaf and circular fillings. The motif may be used for a greetings card or mounted onto a needle case. (PATTERN DESIGNED AND WORKED BY ANGELA THOMPSON)

PREPARING THE PATTERN OUTLINE, METHOD 2

This method is described on page 16. The use of the blue sticky-backed film is suitable for patterns measuring up to 23cm (9in) each way.

BASTING THE BRAID IN POSITION

Prepare a piece of braid about 56cm (22in) in length (extra braid is allowed for joining). Fasten on the braid at the base of the left-hand leaf, but above the lower edge. Leave the braid tail-thread for joining later. Using the ladder stitch, baste the braid to the background, following the pattern outlines and easing the braid around the curve. At the leaf point, crease the braid between finger and thumb to make a sharp bend, but do not overlap. Sew down by angling the stitches from the centre point outwards, in a fan shape (see fig. 53).

Continue around the bottom curve until the right-hand leaf point is reached, then work back to the leaf base. Curve the braid at the bottom and sew up the stem. The flower petals are sewn down next. Do not pull the braid tightly, but ease around the fullness of the curves. When the three petals are sewn in place, coil the remainder of the braid around the circle, working in a clockwise direction from the base of the last petal (see fig. 54).

JOINING THE BRAID ENDS

When the circle is completed, unravel the end of the braid far enough to fit against the final petal loop. Leave enough thread to pass through the crochet loops of the braid to secure them before sewing the braid end to the picot loops on the circle. Join the starting end of the braid at the base of the leaf in a similar manner.

SEWING THE BRAID JOINS

Using a strong thread in a matching colour, join the braids wherever they touch by oversewing through the picot loops. Alternatively use a ladder stitch. When one section is completed, pass the needle through the braid to the next joining position. First, join the base of the stem to each of the leaves, where they touch, and then join the stem to the circle. Finish by joining the petals to each other and to the circle (see fig. 55).

WORKING THE PATTERN

Lay the foundation threads within the petal shapes, leaf shapes and the circle, ready to work the chosen fillings. When all is finished, remove the lace by snipping the ladder stitch threads from the back of the pattern support with pointed scissors. Do not cut from the front.

Filling Stitches used on the completed flower motif, fig. 56, are as follows:

Outer petals	arabesque
Middle petal	arched centre
Centre circle	backstitch wheel
Leaves	feather stitch

SIMPLE PATTERNS FOR SMALL ITEMS

The items in this section have been designed and worked by Kathleen Waller.

Celtic patterns

It is seldom that two patterns completely alike are found in Romanian point lace. Either the workers have a large supply of traditional patterns to call on, or they are gifted in producing so many different designs. Even when the pattern outline is the same, the fillings and treatment can be entirely different. It is this variety of pattern and often-unexpected use of fillings or braid that gives the lace its vitality.

Many of the laces have intricate pattern elements, but simple designs are equally effective. As in other tape laces, the outlines are decorative as well as functional. The braid can be used purely as an outline or interlaced to form an integral part of the design. Celtic patterns, famous for interlacing elements, are easy to adapt for Romanian point lace, providing they are not too complicated.

The interlaced motifs have been adapted from traditional Celtic patterns to make a needlework set comprising pincushion, needle case and scissors keeper. The worker can choose any suitable fillings or use the ones illustrated. These patterns are suitable for beginners and, when finished, will either make a useful addition to the lace worker's accessories or serve as a gift for a special friend.

Crossed interlacing

This pattern, which is used for the scissors keeper, is worked as four separate sections. Start at one of the intersections and proceed by sewing down the braid up to the next intersection. Cut the braid and finish off the end. Continue on the other side of the intersection and complete the loop. Repeat with the remaining two sections. Join in the braid ends at all four junctions and work the fillings. When these are finished, remove from the pattern support and sew onto the scissors pad.

Filling stitches used on this motif, illustrated in fig. 59, are as follows:

Outer sections	obelisk
Centre circle	windmill sails

Diagram 53: Crossed interlacing

FIGURE 57: Triple leaf on a pincushion

FIGURE 58: Interlacing on a needle case

FIGURE 59: Crossed interlacing on a scissors keeper

TRIPLE LEAF

This little pattern, which is applied to the pincushion, is formed from four separate sections of braid. The method for laying down the braid is similar to that used on the previous 'crossed interlacing' pattern. Join at the intersections in the usual way. Alternatively, it is possible to use one continuous length of braid for this or any similar Celtic interlaced pattern, instead of cutting at the intersections. Follow the working method for interlacing detailed below.

Filling stitches used on this motif, illustrated in fig. 57, are as follows:

Top leaf	obelisk
Side sections	decorative curve
Centre	windmill sails

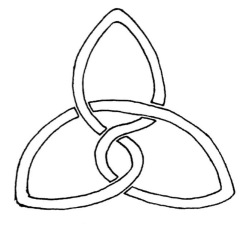

DIAGRAM 54: Triple leaf

INTERLACING

Two separate lengths of braid are woven under and over one another according to the pattern, without the cut joins seen in the previous two examples. It may be easier for a beginner to lay down one of the braid sections completely, leaving spaces between the basting stitches, where appropriate, to allow room for the interlacing. This may occur where the braid weaves under and over itself, or when the second braid section is, in its turn, sewn into position. Join at the intersections in the usual way.

Filling stitches used on this motif, illustrated in fig. 58, are as follows:

Top and bottom	obelisk
Two sides	windmill sails

DIAGRAM 55: Interlacing

GREETINGS AND ANNIVERSARY CARDS

Simple motifs will give the beginner practice in lace-making before embarking on a more complicated project. The patterns for these small gift cards may, at some later date, be incorporated in a larger piece. If necessary, the finished motifs can be stiffened using one of the methods detailed on page 84. They are held to the face of the card mount with a colourless fabric adhesive. The glue is placed under the braid areas only, using just sufficient to secure the motif in position without marking the face of the card mount. Alternatively, cut small pieces of double-sided sticky tape.

SYMMETRICAL DOODLE

This small motif is made from one piece of braid. The 'start' and 'finish' positions are shown in diagram 56. The braid outlines of the lower sections are placed close together. There is no room for a filling stitch, so the top and bottom braids are sewn together with an overcasting stitch, the thread being taken through the picot loops on both edges. The motif has been worked in a shaded thread, but would look equally attractive in a plain colour.

Filling stitches used on this motif, illustrated in fig. 60, are as follows:

Top section   single feather stitch on herringbone

FIVE-PETAL FLOWER

Start by basting the stalk into position before working around the curved petals. This motif has been worked in a single colour, but would look equally good in a shaded or glitter thread for a Christmas or other special card. The foundation loops for the centre filling are sewn into the bases of the five petals.

Filling stitches used on this motif, illustrated in fig. 61, are as follows:

Flower petals   double buttonhole on herringbone
Flower centre   star loops

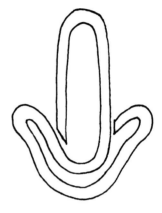

DIAGRAM 56: Symmetrical doodle

DIAGRAM 57: Five-petal flower

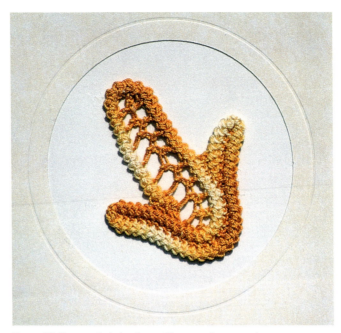

FIGURE 60: Symmetrical doodle motif mounted on a card

FIGURE 61: Five-petal flower mounted on a card

FIGURE 62: Bird on a branch featured on a card

FIGURE 63: Cockerel featured on a card

BIRD DESIGNS

The pattern for the bird-on-a-branch motif has been adapted from the outlines illustrated on a little gift tag that came from the Czech Republic. The cockerel design is one commonly found in Central European countries, often depicted on painted furniture and pottery, or incorporated into embroidery and lace. Another familiar design, showing pairs of birds facing each other, crossed the Atlantic with settlers from Europe and became part of the American folk art tradition. Any of these simple bird outlines can be adapted easily for Romanian point lace. They are suitable for cards of all types or can be mounted as small pictures.

COCKEREL

Start at the base of the bird, where the feet join, and ladder-stitch the braid in place. Take care to keep to the outlines of the comb on top of the head and around the heart shape on the body.

Filling stitches used on this motif, illustrated in fig. 63, are as follows:

Body	chain on ladder foundation and double buttonhole on ladder foundation
Heart shape	fan weave
Feet	whipped bars

BIRD ON A BRANCH

The bird outline is made from one continuous piece of braid. Start in the body centre with the wing outline, work up to the tail, curve back again for the body and head, then curve down to the lower body and back up to the two tail pieces. Join at the side and sew the fork of the tail to the body. Ladder-stitch a piece of brown or fawn-coloured braid in position for the branch.

Each leg is formed by laying two threads in position, then filling with simple needle-weaving. The claws are worked as whipped bars sewn over the branch. The little beak is added afterwards as a wrapped picot loop. A simple herringbone stitch in contrasting thread is worked over zigzag bars as a filling for this motif, illustrated in fig. 62.

DIAGRAM 58: Cockerel

DIAGRAM 59: Bird on a branch

TWO BOOKMARKS

A long item, such as a bookmark, will give further practice in sewing down the braid outlines and working different filling stitches. Both bookmarks were made with a no. 20 crochet thread. Avoid thicker threads or the bookmark will be too bulky. Both bookmarks will shrink in size when removed from the pattern support. Allowance has been made for this.

The lace can be set by ironing between a towel and a damp cloth, but avoid using too much pressure, or the lace may become distorted.

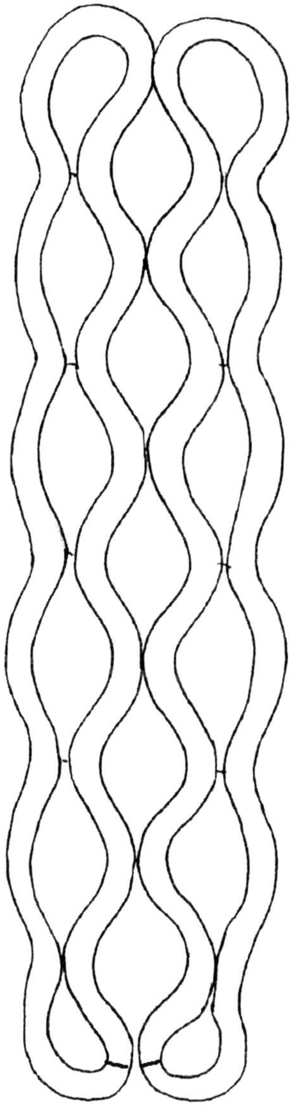

DIAGRAM 60: Bookmark 1 – circle column

DIAGRAM 61 : Bookmark 2 – twin hearts

BOOKMARK 1 – CIRCLE COLUMN

This pattern is formed by two separate loops of braid, joined in the centre where they touch. The starting place for each loop is at the base of the pattern. Sew the braid picots together at each joining point before beginning the filling stitches, which are confined to the central part of the bookmark. The positions for the whipped bars are not marked on the pattern. If these are to be worked, draw them in with a pencil first, then ink in afterwards. Many of the filling stitches described in the previous sections can be used as alternatives to those listed below.

Filling stitches used on this bookmark, illustrated in fig. 64, are as follows:

Centre circles	windmill sails
	Brussels lace circle
	backstitch wheel
Outer sections	whipped bars

FIGURE 64: Circle column

BOOKMARK 2 – TWIN HEARTS

Each heart motif is worked as a separate unit with a double outline of braid, which is joined at the lower point. The braid outlines at the sides, which loop around to make the inner circles, are joined to the outer braid of the heart motif. Sew the inner circles together where they link in the middle and to themselves where they touch at the side. The positions for the whipped bars are not marked on the pattern. If these are to be worked, draw them in with a pencil first, then ink in afterwards.

Filling stitches used on this bookmark, illustrated in fig. 65, are as follows:

Heart centres	arched centre
Heart borders	buttonhole on ladder foundation
Circle centres	windmill sails

FIGURE 65: Twin hearts

CHAPTER 9
IDEAS FOR THE FESTIVE SEASON

CHRISTMAS TREE ORNAMENTS

Laces and braids have innumerable uses for the festive season, including ornaments, gifts, cards and finishing touches to the Christmas table. The items in the following selection of Christmas tree ornaments are quick to work and can be used year after year.

STIFFENING THE MOTIFS

All motifs for the tree will need to be stiffened if they are to hang properly. The Romanian Lace Group stiffened all their finished lace after it had been washed, using a boiled sugar-water solution. Use one measure of sugar to one measure of hot water. Make sure the sugar is thoroughly dissolved, then let it cool before dipping the lace.

An alternative way of stiffening the fabric is to use PVA craft medium (white glue), diluted one part of medium to four of water. Both methods work well, but note that articles stiffened in either of these ways may become limp when exposed to damp conditions.

There are several commercial fabric stiffeners on the market, including Moravia Decoration Starch, which is made in Denmark. The decoration starch is not water soluble, which allows the stiffened articles to hold their shape. One part of starch is mixed with one part of water and brushed or sponged onto the lace shape, after which any surplus is taken off with a paper towel. A flat motif can be laid to dry on a sheet of plastic, but 3D items need to be supported on a bottle top or suitable former. Dry the lace immediately, using a hairdryer. It is the heat that fixes and sets the starch.

Make sure that any stiffening agent is not readily flammable before using it on items such as Christmas tree ornaments.

BRAID-DECORATED BALLS

Lace-covered baubles make excellent ornaments for the Christmas tree. This is where the use of colour and glitter threads comes into its own. A decorative braid, placed around the circumference of a silk-thread ball, is held in place with a lacing stitch. Two crochet-covered rings are worked first and temporarily held to the top and bottom of the ball with pins or glued into place with a non-flammable adhesive. The crochet braid is pinned around the middle and the ends are then joined neatly. A glitter thread is laced between the points of the braid and the loops of the crochet rings. The lacing patterns can be varied for each ball. Finally, make a hanging loop and fasten to the top.

Braids 3 and 4 both work well on items such as the small ornamental balls (see pages 64–5 for instructions). For the larger silk-covered balls, choose braid 6 (see instructions on page 67). Candlelight brand metallic threads and a mixture of a metallic thread and crochet cotton are used to decorate the Christmas tree ornaments. The circular ring, shown on page 91, has been decorated with little red beads combined with green threads to suggest a holly wreath, while glitter-thread braid is used to outline a heart motif, the braid being held in place with a lacing stitch.

The items in this section have been designed and worked by Kathleen Waller.

CROCHET BELLS

These little bells are worked in a glitter thread. Candlelight was used here, but it is worth experimenting with other metallic threads to find the best result.

Start with eleven chain. Miss one chain, one dc (sc) into each of next nine chain.

Three dc (sc) into the last chain and nine dc (sc) down the second side of the starting chain.

From now on work dc (sc) into the back of the loops.

Turn. One chain, four dc (sc). Sl st into the next stitch.

Turn. One chain, four dc (sc) to the end.

Turn. One chain, ten dc (sc). Three dc (sc) into the next stitch, i.e. around the top, and dc (sc) to the end.

Turn. One chain, four dc (sc). Sl st into the next stitch.

Turn. One chain, four dc (sc) to the end.

Turn. One chain, one dc (sc) into each stitch along one side, around the curve at the top and down the other side.

Finish off, leaving 15–20cm (about 6–8in) of thread for joining this section to the next. Work two more sections and join to form a bell. Join the thread at the base of the bell and work dc (sc) all around to make a smooth finish. Stiffen according to the instructions on page 84. Attach a loop of thread to the top, ready for hanging on the Christmas tree (see the finished bells illustrated on page 91).

CROCHET LEAF

The crochet leaf motif is included here because it is worked in a similar way to the sections that form the crochet bells. Crochet leaf patterns are worked in many countries, including Ireland, where the traditional Irish crochet found favour during the latter part of the 19th century. The leaf is a popular motif in Romanian point lace. It is used to accompany the bullion knot grapes, either featured on its own or joined with a flower to make a decoration for dress and accessories.

Start with sixteen chain.

One dc (sc) into the second chain from the hook. One dc (sc) into each chain up to the last. Three dc (sc) into this.

Thirteen dc (sc) down the second side of the starting chain. Three dc (sc) into the chain-loop.

Working into the back of each loop from now on, twelve dc (sc).

In subsequent rows, work three dc (sc) into the middle dc (sc) of the three dc (sc).

Turn. One chain, miss first dc (sc), work dc (sc) to within three dc (sc) at the top of the leaf segment.

* One chain, turn, miss one dc (sc), work to within two chain and turning chain.*

Repeat from * to * twice.

One chain, turn. Miss one dc (sc), work to the base of the leaf and finish with a sl st.

Make two further pieces, join and form a stem by making a chain and working dc (sc) along the length.

Five of these sections joined will make a complete unit, as used to decorate the fabric-covered box lid illustrated on page 126.

FIGURE 66 Top row: stages in making the sections for the crochet bell. Bottom row: a crochet leaf worked in a similar way

FIGURE 67: Crochet leaf motifs are combined with grapes on a long, narrow mat from western Romania (ANGELA THOMPSON COLLECTION)

SIX FLAT BELLS FOR THE CHRISTMAS TREE

Although these little bells have been designed to hang on the Christmas tree, they would look equally attractive hanging in a window or mounted on wires and assembled as a mobile hanging.

An individual bell pattern can make an excellent insert for a Christmas or wedding card. Use the pattern singly, or with pairs of bells mounted with the front one overlapping the other slightly. A 'ring' of bells, like the ones in fig. 68, would decorate a Christmas table setting, with smaller ones as guest place markers. Finally, individual bells make lovely gift tags to mark a birthday, or could be made in gold or silver thread for a special anniversary.

FIGURE 68: Ring of bells

These flat bell motifs have been worked in a no. 20 crochet thread, either in a plain colour or in a shaded thread. Little beads, threaded in a variety of ways, have been added to the base of the bells to indicate the clapper. Beads add sparkle to motifs and tiny beads decorate the centre-ring filling of one particular bell.

FLAT BELL PATTERNS

The bell decorations have been adapted from bobbin lace patterns, and each bell is made from a continuous piece of braid. Many traditional lace patterns can be used for Romanian point, but may need some alteration to accommodate the various filling stitches. The patterns for the six little bells are shown in diagrams 62 a, b, c, d, e and f on the following page.

The bells shown in diagram 62 a, d, e and f have the braid ends sewn to the inside curve of the bell, while bells in diagrams 62 b and c have ends that join within the pattern. Sew the braid ends as neatly as possible – these little bells will be seen from both sides when they are hanging from the tree.

Filling stitches and braid patterns used on the bells illustrated in fig. 68 are as follows:

a	diagram 62a	centre	buttonhole ring
b	diagram 62b	centre	buttonhole on ladder
c	diagram 62c	centre	arched centre
d	diagram 62d	sides	decorative weave 1 (p.40)
e	diagram 62e	sides	interweave thread
f	diagram 62f	centre	star loops

The bead decorations and clappers are added as the braids are joined and the fillings made.

One method of making the clappers is to fasten on to the base of the bell and thread on a number of small beads, taking the thread through a larger bead at the bottom, back up through the first set of beads and then fastening off. A beaded loop can be made in a similar way, but a second set of smaller beads is threaded after the central bead and finished back at the base of the bell. A third way is to thread on three larger beads, then several small beads, one large bead at the bottom, through the same number of small beads again, then back up through the large beads.

Stiffen the lace bells according to the instructions on page 84.

DIAGRAM 62: a

DIAGRAM 62: b

DIAGRAM 62: c

DIAGRAM 62: d

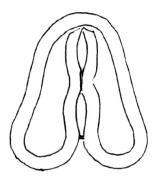

DIAGRAM 62: e

DIAGRAM 62: f

FIGURE 69: Six little bells on the Christmas tree (PHOTOGRAPHY BY BOB CHALLINOR)

FIGURE 70: Christmas tree decorations (PHOTOGRAPHY BY BOB CHALLINOR)

PLACE MATS

The traditional technique of Romanian point lace is frequently used to produce large lace items, such as mats, tablecloths and chair covers. The lace looks equally good worked as a smaller motif or edging mounted on a contrasting background fabric. The following pattern motifs for place mats are worked in plain and shaded threads. The corner designs have been applied to one corner only, but the motif could be applied to the opposite corners and the edging pattern may be sewn to both ends if required. A corner can be designed as a repeat pattern for a border, or a border pattern motif adapted for a corner. It is worth taking the time to experiment with pattern variations to help to enlarge a design collection.

FLOWER AND LEAF – PLACE MAT CORNER

Outlines in fawn-coloured thread tone with the natural linen of the place mat, while the blue thread provides a contrast. Different colour combinations can alter the look of a design by emphasizing certain areas, although the basic pattern may remain the same.

INVERTED HEARTS – PLACE MAT CORNER

The linen place mat is decorated with a border pattern comprising little heart motifs. When inverted, these alternate to form a second set of heart motifs. Whipped bars hold together the space at the corner between the motifs. Some corners are not easy to design. Hold a mirror at a 45-degree angle against a row of motifs to find the best place to turn the corner.

PLACE MATS – EDGING PATTERN

The fillings for motifs used in the edging pattern comprise buttonhole rings and whipped bars, some with a picot, some without.

The little buttonhole-covered rings are worked first. See pages 52 and 53 for instructions. Baste the completed ring into the centre of the motif before working the connecting whipped bars.

MAKING THE MAT

Use old bleached linen or a similar fabric and turn down the hems with mitred corners for neatness. When cutting the fabric, make allowances for turning a double hem on all four sides. For example, add 4cm ($1^1/_2$ in) to the overall measurements for a 1cm ($^1/_2$ in) hem. Instructions for withdrawing the threads and making mitred corners can be found in basic sewing books, or consult *Mary Thomas's Embroidery Book*. Alternatively, apply the motifs to purchased table mats.

MOUNTING LACE EDGINGS

When mounting a lace edging, place right sides together and seam stitch (a very fine oversewing stitch), working through each loop on the braid edge. For a motif, place it in the required position on the mat and stitch through the braid loops to the fabric background with the same thread as used for the braid. The finished place mats, with hand-worked hemstitch and mitred corners, are illustrated on page 143.

Diagram 63: Flower and leaf corner design

FIGURE 71: Place mat with flower and leaf corner

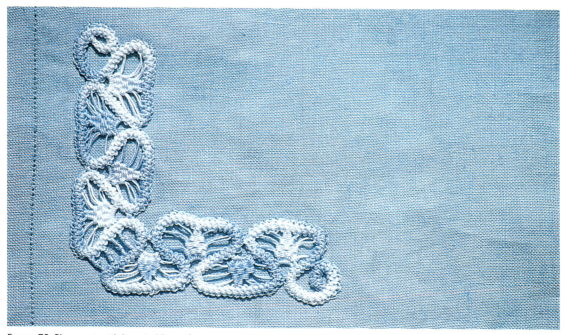

FIGURE 72: Place mat with 'inverted hearts' corner

Filling stitches used on the flower and leaf corner motif:

Flower petals   divided wheat ear
Leaf shapes   herringbone lacing

Filling used on the 'inverted hearts' corner motif:

Heart shapes   pyramid basket
Corner   whipped bars

Fillings used for the place mat edging:
Leaf shapes   whipped bars and picot bars

FIGURE 73: Place mat with edging pattern

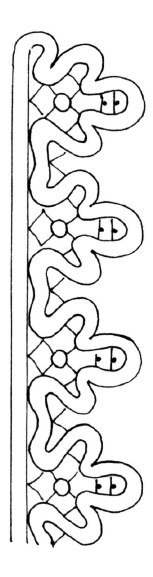

DIAGRAM 64 : Edging pattern

DIAGRAM 65: Inverted hearts

COASTERS AND PAPERWEIGHTS

Most of the small pattern motifs used on greetings cards are equally suitable for mounting under coasters and paperweights, providing that they are not too bulky. Most paperweights have a recessed base, allowing space for heavier items, but the plastic mounts made for glass coasters require a flat item as decoration.

COASTER 1

Coaster mounts vary, but the circular ones illustrated are made in transparent plastic. They come in two parts, with a card backing placed on the top of the circular base. The finished motif is fixed on top of this card and the completed base pressed into the top. A piece of felt or other suitable non-fray fabric may be substituted instead of the backing card. Instructions for assembly are usually included with the coaster.

Fillings used for coaster 1:

Top shape	arched centre
Side	whipped bars
Sides	woven wheels
Stem	centre weave

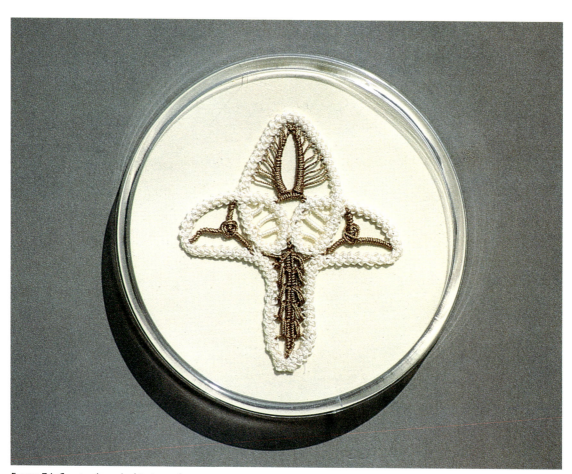

FIGURE 74: Coaster 1, worked in two colours

COASTER 2

The motif for the second coaster is worked in a turquoise thread. Some people prefer the traditional white, but the use of colour in lace is not a modern innovation – many of the Central European and Russian lace makers have long made use of red, combined with the fawn of natural linen threads.

Fillings used for coaster 2:

Side petal shape	whipped bars
Centre/top petal	circular interweave
Stem	herringbone lacing

PAPERWEIGHTS

For an easy way to mount a motif in the base of the paperweight use felt or a similar non-fray material, cut to the correct size. Fix the motif on the felt, either by using a small dab of craft glue or with a few strategically placed stitches. The mounted base is then attached to the paperweight with a thin film of the same glue. A matching decorative braid may be fixed around the sides to make a pleasing finish.

A glass paperweight with lace decoration is included in the illustration on page 142.

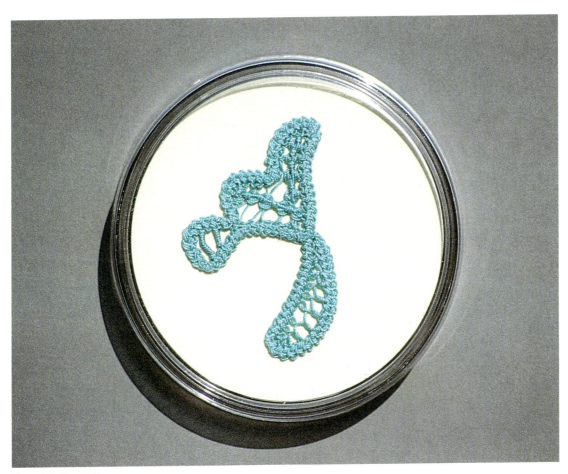

FIGURE 75: Coaster 2

DIAGRAM 66: Pattern for coaster 1

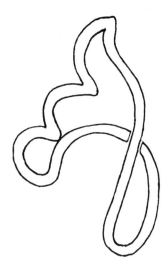

DIAGRAM 67: Pattern for coaster 2

CHAPTER 10
PATTERN DESIGN AND ADAPTATION

Many lace makers are happy to work from a selection of patterns designed exclusively for their own particular type of lace. This leaves a whole design source untouched. A variety of other laces are suitable for adaptation to Romanian point lace, while design outlines can be traced from simple motifs found in children's books, or taken from books with design ideas produced for other crafts. There are several ways of making pattern drawing easier. One is the use of polar graph paper. This is helpful when planning a circular design, such as the five- or six-petal flower, a popular motif frequently incorporated into Romanian lace.

Draw the design in pencil and, when satisfactory, copy it on tracing paper. The pencil lines can be rubbed out and the graph paper used again. The flower motifs worked from these patterns can be found on pages 50 and 51.

DIAGRAM 68: Six-petal flower drawn on polar graph paper

DIAGRAM 69: Three-heart pattern traced from drawing on polar graph paper

FIGURE 76: *Russian angel from the Vologda region, north of Moscow (VOLOGDA LACE FROM THE ANGELA THOMPSON COLLECTION)*

Figure 77: Romanian angel (Designed and worked by Angela Thompson)

DIAGRAM 70: Pattern for the Romanian angel; the finished lace is designed to be mounted as a picture

ADAPTING A DESIGN FROM A BOBBIN LACE PATTERN

The 'Russian angel' on page 102 was purchased from a group of lace workers on the shores of the Rybinsk reservoir, part of the Russian waterways complex that joins Moscow to Saint Petersburg and then to the North Sea. In spite of the cold, the women were sitting out in the open, working with large wooden bobbins on bolster pillows. This northern region is famous for the Vologda laces, which feature intricate snowflake designs and border patterns of convoluted tape. At one time, these lace borders were sewn to the hems of the petticoats worn for display by a prospective bride. The larger the number of lace hems, the greater the status of the bride. Unlike the true tape laces, which are assembled from separate parts, the bobbin tapes are worked as one piece, the meandering designs being linked together where they meet by the means of 'sewings', which form part of the bobbin lace structure.

PLANNING THE DESIGN

The original Russian angel lace motif was photocopied first so that the design outline could be traced from the photocopy. The final pattern draft was covered with blue matte film for the backing support. When planning a design, it is a good idea to wind a piece of crochet braid around the pattern outline to see which is the best route to take, with as few joins as possible. Alternatively, draw the new outline on the photocopy with a coloured fibre-tipped pen.

The body line was altered to accommodate the crochet braids chosen to represent the feathery texture of the wings. The basic braid outlines the body area and includes the flower motif on the skirt as part of the structure. A lacy braid outlines the crown headdress and the lower skirt-frill, while a more decorative braid has been used for the dress border. Little buttonhole rings cover the wing intersections and add emphasis to the crown.

The basic braid takes in the head, body, skirt and flower motif as one continuous length. It is joined at the top of the head with the ends hidden under the crown. Cut the fancy braid pieces to length and neaten before basting in place. The ends can be hidden under the basic braid where necessary. The whipped bars and circle motifs are added after the fillings have been worked, while the buttonhole rings are sewn on last of all. The finished lace is sewn to a firm fabric, which is stretched over a card former and laced across the back, both ways.

Fillings used for the Romanian angel pattern:

Headdress	wrapped fan filling
Wing tops	arabesque
Wing ends	herringbone lacing
Skirt flower	obelisk
Flower centre	star loops
Skirt frill	ziggurat
Skirt borders	petal weave

Braids used:

Body outline	braid 1
Headdress and skirt frill	braid 2
Wings	braid 4
Skirt band	braid 6

FIGURE 78: Tea-cosy cover in Battenburg tape lace (ANGELA THOMPSON COLLECTION)

FIGURE 79: Tea cosy cover in Romanian point lace (GEORGE BUTTERS COLLECTION)

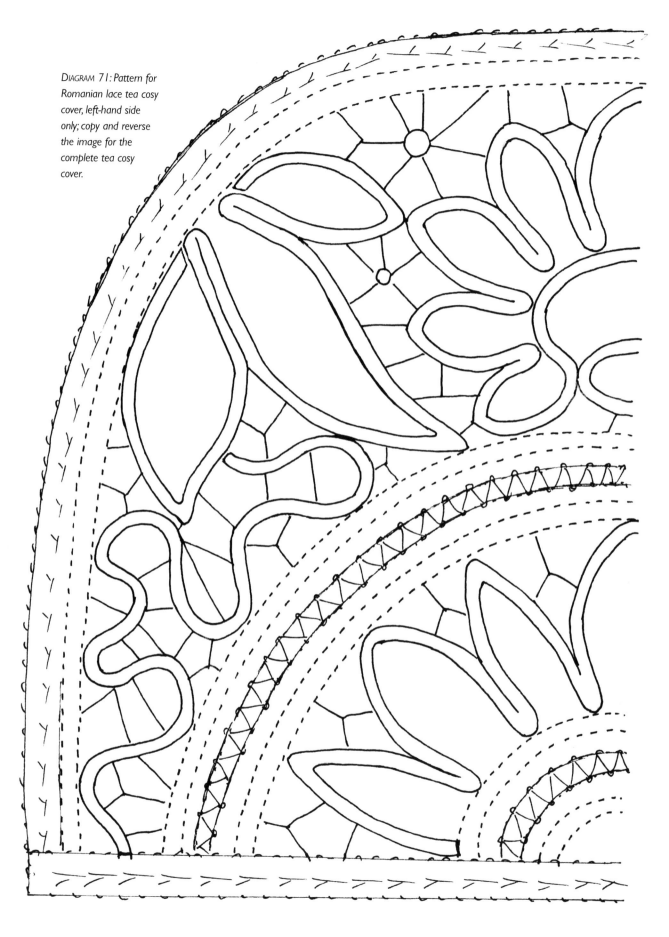

DIAGRAM 71: Pattern for Romanian lace tea cosy cover, left-hand side only; copy and reverse the image for the complete tea cosy cover.

A DESIGN FROM BATTENBURG TAPE LACE

Tape laces were at their height of popularity at the end of the 19th century. This followed a revival of amateur interest in the heavy guipure laces. Reproductions were made of 17th-century Venetian needlepoint lace, but this required both skill and the availability of ample leisure time. The early bobbin tape laces of the Flemish type were much easier to copy. Some of these revival laces were made with decorative manufactured tapes and included a variety of needlelace fillings, many of them common to Romanian point.

The Battenburg tape laces are simple in form, relying on the circular coils of woven braid to give direction to the pattern. Fillings include herringbone, woven wheels, twisted bars, buttonhole rings and a few needlelace stitches. The Battenburg tea cosy cover illustrated on page 106, was probably made in China, where they have been making reproduction laces for a number of years as an export commodity for the Western market.

The original Battenburg lace cover was first photocopied (note that if a design is symmetrical, it is only necessary to reproduce half of the pattern). The photocopy was sent to Romania for members of the Lace Group to interpret and work as Romanian point lace. It is interesting to note that the workers have not made an exact copy of the original design, but rather taken the main design elements and reinterpreted them in their own tradition.

The finished lace is in two colours, natural and a mushroom beige. The wide curve on the original front is repeated by incorporating a fancy-braid that is bordered by the basic braids and held in place with herringbone stitch. The lower motif has been followed, incorporating braid and a variety of fillings. The upper flower is smaller, and leaf shapes have been introduced. All the motifs are connected with whipped bars, some with woven-wheel intersections.

WORKING THE LACE

Sew all the basic braid outlines first, then lay the fancy braid in position and baste. Work the fillings next, including those from the original cosy or ones of personal choice. A few of the fillings are not included in this book – there are countless variations, and individual workers adapt stitch patterns for their personal use. Choose braids of the appropriate width. A single wide braid is used to join the two cosy parts together and to go around the lower hem. Ease the braid around the curve and oversew the braid edges together through the picot loops. The finished tea cosy cover is mounted over an inner pad made in a contrasting colour.

Fillings used on the tea cosy cover:

Flower petals	divided wheat ear
	feather variations, mirrored
	alternating needle-weave
Leaf shapes	plaited feather stitch
	interweave on double thread
	alternating buttonhole

FIGURE 80: Butterfly I (DESIGNED AND WORKED BY ANGELA THOMPSON)

FIGURE 81: Detail of upper wing

FIGURE 82: Detail of lower wing and body

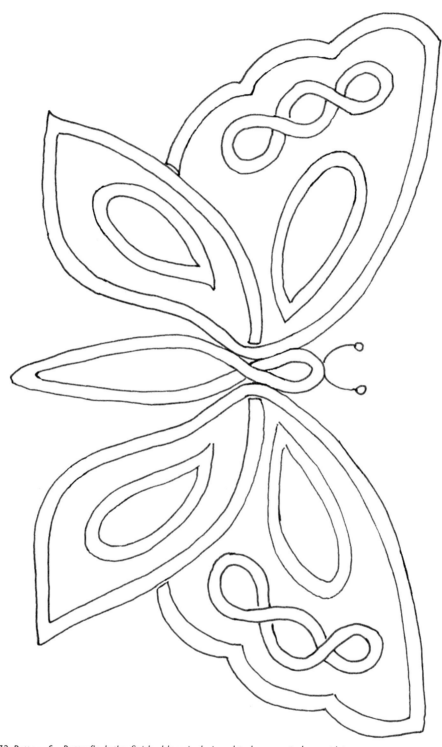

DIAGRAM 72: Pattern for Butterfly 1; the finished lace is designed to be mounted as a picture

BUTTERFLY DESIGNS

The butterfly has for centuries been a favourite motif in lace, embroidery and other textile crafts. In Oriental art the butterfly signified both longevity and marital felicity , so it was included in both Chinese and Japanese embroidery. The butterfly motif is also prominent in several European laces. These include the butterfly pattern in Cluny-type laces, with its half-stitch wings and raised tally for the body, the three-dimensional butterflies in Brussels *point de gaze* needlepoint laces, the delicate butterflies in black Chantilly bobbin lace, the butterflies that feature in East Midlands point and plaited laces, in Devon part-lace from Honiton and in many of the tape laces, including Branscombe point. Members of the Romanian Lace Group produce separate butterfly motifs (Figure 85). They are charming creatures, with oval wings, double figure-of-eight bodies and huge eyes made from buttonhole rings.

BUTTERFLY 1

Trace off or photocopy the pattern. Using the basic braid, lay the figure-of-eight shape for the head and body onto the pattern support. Hide the ends underneath the crossing and ladder-stitch in place. The fancy braid outline for the upper and lower wing sections is formed on each side by a separate length of braid. Start at the body-head intersection, then go down and around the outer border of the lower wing. Come up to the intersection again, continuing around the upper wing and finishing part-way along the lower wing top. Sew all wing-braid joins together.

Next, make basic braid loops to the correct size for the wing decorations. Sew the ends together neatly, then baste them into position. Hide the join of the figure-of-eight wing decoration underneath one of the crossings.

Work the body and head filling first. Using the same colour as the braid, lay a ladder of bars and work two mirrored rows of feather stitch groups, each time starting from the base. Work the wing fillings next, and then the circle fillings inside the figure-of-eight. Finally, lace the braid shapes to the outer wings with herringbone stitch, working into every zigzag point of the outer braid. Even-out the placing of the herringbone stitches into the picots on the braid loops – it is necessary to be 'creative' at the corners and where the shape narrows. The little antennae are made by taking a length of thin wire, doubling it to join in the middle and twisting the side ends into tiny loops. Bind all with a coloured thread, from the middle to the top loop, around the loop and back to the middle. Repeat for the other side. Leave a thread end and sew the wire base behind the head top.

Fillings used in Butterfly 1:

Body and head	feather stitch groups
Top wings	arabesque
Lower wings	arched centre
Circles	backstitch wheel
Braids used	basic braid 1
	braid 2

FIGURE 83: Butterfly 2 (DESIGNED AND WORKED BY ANGELA THOMPSON)

Figure 84a: Detail of upper wing

Figure 84b: Detail of lower wing and body

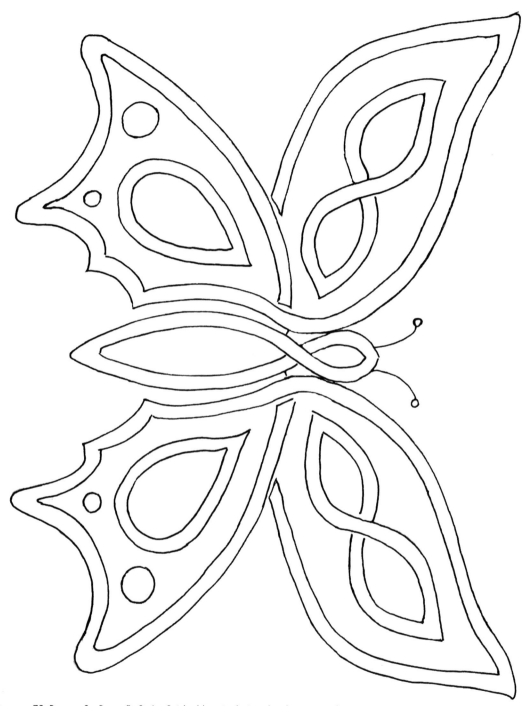

DIAGRAM 73: Pattern for Butterfly 2; the finished lace is designed to be mounted as a picture

BUTTERFLY 2

There are many sources for butterfly design. The wing and body outlines for the two butterflies illustrated were taken from photographs of actual butterflies. The wing patterns have been simplified to accommodate the Romanian lace elements. It is easier to make figure-of-eight shapes than to work separate braid circles for the wing spots.

Apart from the natural history books produced for butterfly identification, many pattern books include butterfly designs with simple outlines that are easy to adapt for the Romanian point laces. The patterns in Dover Publications are free of copyright, while the delightful reprint of *The Schole-house for the Needle*, originally published in 1632, has several butterfly drawings in the embroidery section, as well as plants and flowers. During the 16th century, butterflies were often included in Elizabethan embroidery, being worked in tent stitch on canvas or embroidered in silks as dress decoration. The designs for these appear in several recently published books on historical embroidery and are suitable for adaptation as lace patterns.

MAKING THE LACE

Prepare the pattern as usual and lay the figure-of-eight braid shape for the head and body on the pattern support. Ladder-stitch in place. The fancy braid outline for the upper and lower wing sections is formed on each side by a separate length of braid. Start at the body-head intersection, then go down and around the outer border of the lower wing. Come up to the intersection again, continuing around the upper wing and finishing part-way along the lower wing top. Sew all wing-braid joins together. Next, make basic braid loops to the correct size for the wing decorations. Sew the ends together neatly, then baste into position.

Work the body and head filling first. Using the same colour as the braid, lay a ladder of bars and cover with plaited feather stitch. This stitch was chosen to simulate the furry hairs. Work the wing fillings next and then baste the buttonhole rings into position. Finally, lace the braid shapes to the outer wings with herringbone stitch, working into every zigzag point of the crochet braid on one side and into the braid picots on the opposite side. Even-out the stitches and incorporate the buttonhole rings as the work progresses. The little antennae are made as before, by taking a length of thin wire, doubling it, twisting the ends into tiny loops, and then binding with coloured thread.

Fillings used in Butterfly 2:

Body and head	plaited feather stitch, single
Top wings	asymmetric curve
	plain wheat ear
Lower wings	fancy arched centre
	buttonhole rings
Braids used	basic braid 1
	braid 2

FIGURE 85: Two Romanian point lace butterflies made by the Romanian Lace Group
(GEORGE BUTTERS COLLECTION)

FIGURE No. 86: A table setting comprising place mats, serving mats and glass mats
(PHOTOGRAPHY BY BOB CHALLINOR, TABLE MATS FROM THE COLLECTION OF GEORGE BUTTERS)

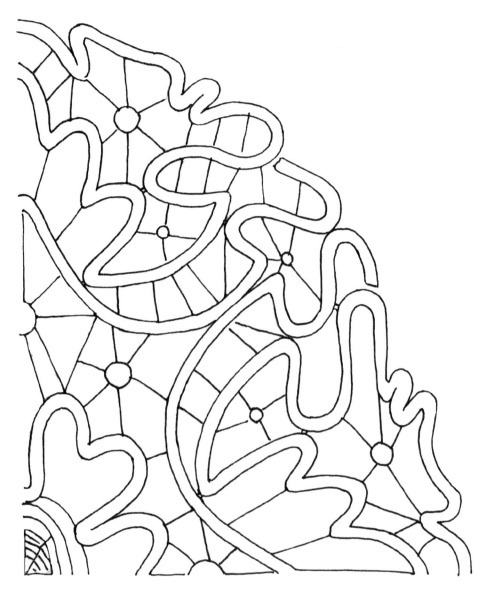

DIAGRAM 74: Pattern for the oval serving mat; only a quarter of the mat is shown in the pattern.

TABLE SETTING

Romanian point lace is not only suitable for application to a variety of different small items, ranging from greetings cards to needlework accessories, it also has a place in its own right as a furnishing lace. The weight of thread used gives a stability to larger items, such as table mats, chair covers and curtain borders.

The Romanians love to decorate their homes. This is part of a long tradition in which folk art flourished and a young girl would prepare embroidered and lace items for her trousseau. In the apartments belonging to the Romanian lace workers, every possible surface – tables, sideboards, chair backs and arms – was covered with beautiful mats. There would even be a hanging draped over the front of the television set (this would be folded back when necessary to view the screen).

The place mats illustrated on page 119 contain a limited number of design elements, but these are adapted to the shape and size of the different mats. They are worked in two colours, a natural shade and a mushroom beige. Each mat has a central flower motif with heart-shaped flower petals, each heart containing a mirrored filling. Five-lobed leaf groups encompass the central flower motif, and all elements are linked together with whipped bars and woven wheels. The central flower motif on the oval mat has six petals, while the round mat and the glass mat flowers each have four petals.

MAKING THE LACE

Prepare the pattern for the oval and round mats by taking a tracing or photocopy of the quarter section shown, repeating it as a mirror image to obtain half the pattern, then repeating to make the whole pattern. On each mat, start by laying down the outlines of the central flower. The glass mat is formed by this motif alone. Complete the pattern by sewing down the braid outline for the outer border, which also encloses the leaf lobe shapes. Work the flower petal fillings first, then the leaf lobe fillings and the mushroom shapes above. Finally, lay the foundation threads for the joining bars. These are covered with thread in a whipping stitch; woven wheels join the centres where several bars meet.

HANDY HINT: if woven wheels are worked over an odd number of threads, the weaving stitches will appear in the right order.

Filling stitches used on the table setting mats:

Heart petals	decorative curve, mirrored
Flower centres	backstitch wheel, stem stitch wheel
Oval mat centre	windmill sails
Centre leaf	buttonhole groups on herringbone
	needle-weave groups on herringbone
Side leaves	buttonhole groups on herringbone
Mushroom shape	herringbone lacing

FIGURE 87: Oval serving mat (GEORGE BUTTERS COLLECTION)

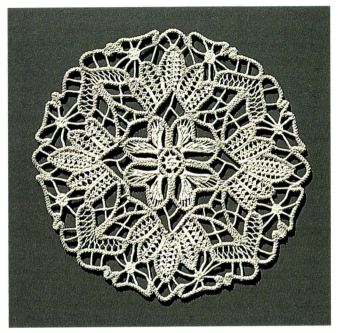

FIGURE 88: Round place mat (George Butters Collection)

FIGURE 89: Flower heart glass mat (George Butters Collection)

DIAGRAM 75: Pattern for the round place mat; only a quarter of the mat is shown in the pattern

DIAGRAM 76: Pattern for the glass mat

FIGURE 90: Romanian point lace motifs applied to two bags. The motifs have been designed to echo the free approach of some of the traditional Romanian lace. Contrasting thread was used for the fillings in one of the bags. A crochet leaf motif has been applied to a fabric-covered box lid. (LACE MOTIFS AND BAGS, CROCHET LEAF AND FABRIC-COVERED BOX DESIGNED AND WORKED BY KATHLEEN WALLER. PHOTOGRAPHY BY BOB CHALLINOR)

FIGURE 91: Detail of the Romanian lace on the cushion illustrated opposite the title page; the central area features interwoven braid (DESIGNED AND WORKED BY KATHLEEN WALLER)

FIGURE 92: A detail of the lace motif applied to the cushion cover; the cushion fillings include asymmetric curve, decorative curve, fancy arched centre, plaited basket, pyramid basket, interwoven bar filling, backstitch and stem stitch wheels, star loops and windmill sails

CHAPTER 11

GALLERY OF TRADITIONAL ROMANIAN POINT LACE

My researches into the different types of Romanian point lace, their design variations, their origins and their location have only just begun. My travels have taken me to Romania and several other European countries, but I shall always treasure my first piece of lace, purchased in the Czech Republic in 1994. It is more open in structure and less stiff than the Romanian lace, but the familiar fillings are there, although worked in a slightly thinner thread.

It was a pleasant surprise to see more examples of this lace at a 'Think Romania' weekend course run by the National Federation of Women's Institutes. A whole selection of lace mats had been given to a tutor on a visit to western Romania, and she was happy to sell some in aid of the orphanages. These lace mats were quite different from the Czech lace. Contrasting colours were used, with a pretty pink and a cream for the braid and the leaf fillings. One is an open lace with large motifs and braid trails, supported by whipped bars and buttonhole rings (see fig. 94).

The first lace mat purchased in Romania was the one displayed on the car outside the monastery. It is a handsome piece, but not worked as firmly as the pieces produced by the Lace Group. The design structure is open, with coiled loops of the foundation braid used to hold the central portion and form a decorative edging. It is the grape and leaf design that gives this mat its special appeal (see figs 98 and 99).

It was interesting to have the 'Romanian' lace from Israel. The first piece comes from Jerusalem. The little grape and crochet leaf motif is very decorative, but the grapes are loosely worked. This does not detract from the piece, and the leaf motif is unusual. The second piece from Israel was quite different, with well-made grapes and a traditional leaf motif, but having five lobes instead of three.

A large lace table mat recently purchased in Zakopane, a resort town in the southern mountain area of Poland, is of particular interest. It was displayed, together with others, on a market stall. After purchasing the mat, I asked through an interpreter where it was made and was told, somewhat reluctantly, that it was not possible to make the lace in Poland for the price they could pay for lace imported across the borders from Romania. Later, I discovered that goods come to Poland from Romania via the Ukraine. The braid on the lace mat is firmly worked and there are some very decorative fillings, but the herringbone lacing in fine thread is rather weak (see fig. 96 on page 132).

The main lace making areas in Romania are in the central mountain region and the western area that was once Transylvania. Jeanmarie Brucia, in an article for *Needle Arts*, December 2001, states that 'macramé lace' is almost unknown in the Moldova and Dobrogea regions of eastern Romania, although crochet and embroidery are popular.

This is borne out by personal experience. Our tour of the monasteries took us to the town of Iaşi in the north-east. It was here that we saw the lace church with the beautiful stonework decoration. There was no Romanian point lace in the costume section of the Ethnographic Museum, nor was it for sale in any of the shops that specialized in embroidery and fine gauze weaving. It did not surprise us that we found no point lace here, for the eastern area is completely different from the mountains we had just left. Gone were the small farmsteads with a patchwork of little fields – instead, vast cooperative farmlands stretched across the flat plains, while in the south, towards the capital, Bucharest, huge factory complexes and oil installations receded into the horizon. It would be interesting to know if the lack of lace making is

Figure 93: Lace mat bought from a market stall in Prague, Czech Republic, 1994 (Angela Thompson Collection)

due to industrialization or whether an area divided from the rest of Romania by the mountain range has a completely different artistic culture.

The items in the lace collection of George Butters, gathered from the central mountain area of Romania, never cease to amaze me. Several of these pieces are illustrated in this section. No two pieces are alike, with regard either to design or to the use of the countless filling stitches. Even items from a 'set' have little differences that give the lace a robust vitality. My admiration for the workers of this delightful lace is boundless. It has given both Kathleen and me great pleasure to discover their stitches and methods, and we hope that others will join us in keeping the tradition alive.

This pointed oval mat is well made, with a firmly worked narrow crochet braid. The pink colour is confined to the fillings in the central flower petals, the circular leaf centres and the decorative braid that outlines the mat. This outer braid is linked to the narrow braid with a herringbone lacing in matching pink.

The circular flower centre is decorated with a double Brussels needlelace stitch, while the pink flower petals are filled with an extended version of ziggurat. The narrow leaves have alternating buttonhole groups, worked over a herringbone foundation. Whipped bars connect the braid trail and the leaf and flower motifs together, as well as giving support to the little buttonhole rings.

The mat measures 55 x 25cm (approx. 22 x 10in).

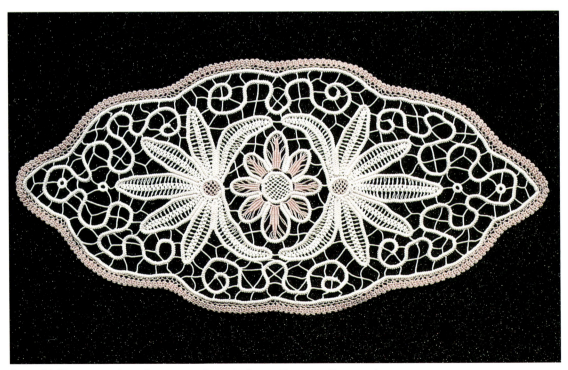

FIGURE 94: Mat in two colours from western Romania (ANGELA THOMPSON COLLECTION)

The centre of interlaced braids is the focal point of this deeply scalloped oval mat. The oval lattice is extended by a border of decorative crochet braid, held in place with herringbone stitch. Arched loops of braid contain ziggurat filling, worked in a dusty pink. These same arched motifs are found on the curved braid sections that form the border of the mat.

Half-flower motifs have double Brussels-stitch centres, worked in cream, while the pink petals are filled with alternating buttonhole groups, worked over a herringbone foundation. Circular flower motifs have a similar centre, but the pink petals are filled with double-plaited feather stitch worked on a ladder of bars.

The mat measures 73 x 35cm (approx. 29 x 14in).

FIGURE 95: *Mat in two colours with lattice centre from western Romania (ANGELA THOMPSON COLLECTION)*

FIGURE 96 : Romanian point lace table mat, bought in Poland, 2002 (ANGELA THOMPSON COLLECTION)

The design for this large table cover consists of curved shapes outlined with a wide decorative braid, linked together with whipped bars and herringbone lacing. The thin lacing thread and the spaces between the bars give the lace an airy appearance, contrasting with the more heavily worked flower-and-leaf motifs. An open edging of narrow braid, twisted into mirrored heart shapes, is connected with whipped bars.

A variety of filling stitches is used, including pyramid basket strung inside the alternate lozenge shapes that are formed by the interlaced braid centre. Whipped thread bars with woven centre joins complete the lattice. Petals are filled with a double plait, and the leaves include buttonhole groups on herringbone and feather stitch variations worked on ladder bars. Buttonhole rings add a decorative element.

The mat measures 91 x 50cm (approx. 36 x 20in).

Six heart-shaped motifs are combined to make the shape of this small mat. It is a good example of the use of decorative crochet braids, worked as an insertion filling for the wide outline of the heart motifs. Each heart is worked as a separate unit before the braid ends are joined together.

Each heart is filled with a spider web of whipped bars held at the centre with a woven wheel. An ordered pattern of bars connects the central flower motif and the flanking leaf patterns. The petals are filled with pyramid basket and the leaf shapes with feather stitch variations on ladder bars.

The mat measures 38 x 23cm (approx. 15 x 9in).

FIGURE 97: *Romanian lace mat, incorporating decorative crochet braids (GEORGE BUTTERS COLLECTION)*

The design elements for this large lace mat are composed solely of the crochet leaf and bullion knot grape motifs. There are no filling stitches, except for the herringbone lacing that holds the braid channels together. A zigzag buttonhole stitch, which is worked over the centre of the herringbone lacing, gives it a degree of stability.

A wider version of the basic crochet braid is used for the looped filling that forms the borders for the central oval and for the scallop-shaped edging. All braid loops are sewn at the intersections, and individual loops are connected with whipped bars.

The mat measures 84 x 58cm (approx. 33 x 23in).

FIGURE 98: Mat purchased outside a monastery, central Romania (ANGELA THOMPSON COLLECTION)

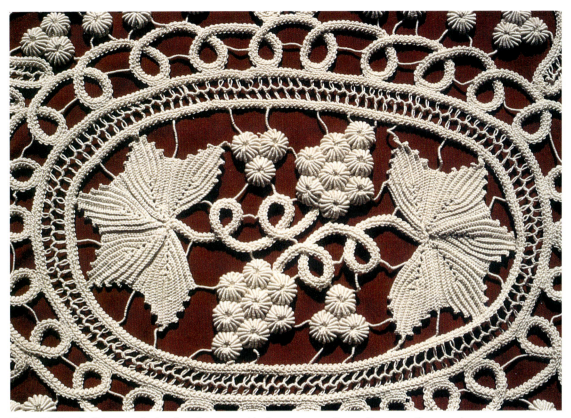

FIGURE 99: Detail of the mat displayed on the car outside the monastery (ANGELA THOMPSON COLLECTION)

The detail shows the central portion of the large lace mat. The individual bullion knot grapes are sewn together at the edges to form grape clusters. In the centre, groups of eight grapes are sewn to stalks made from the looped braid. These are joined at the other end to the crochet leaf motifs, creating a realistic grape vine pattern. Groups of three grapes are held in between by the whipped thread bars to complete the background design.

This little circular mat is an excellent example of the way design is approached in Eastern Europe. There is a spontaneity in the way the plant grows up from the base, barely able to support the larger flower head. Although the scalloped curves of the mat appear similar on both sides, on the right the braid is coiled into a loop, while on the left it forms a little heart motif.

The petal fillings include plaited basket and centre links. A leaf filling has stem-stitch groups worked over ladder bars. Whipped bars, some with woven wheel centres, connect all the design elements together.

The mat is approx. 23cm (9in) in diameter.

FIGURE 100: Circular mat with flower motif (GEORGE BUTTERS COLLECTION)

This little mat contains many of the favourite pattern elements found in Romanian point lace. The central braid lattice is linked with whipped bars, which are joined at the centre and then worked over with windmill sails filling. The four flowers all have petals filled with the centre arch pattern, which forms a delicate repeat pattern on the five curved petals.

The leaf fillings are all worked over ladder bars, which are stitched into every picot. The side leaves use single-plaited feather stitch, while the central leaf features feather-stitch groups worked on alternate groups of the ladder bar threads.

The mat is approx. 25cm (10in) square.

FIGURE 101: Decorative mat with flower-and-leaf borders (GEORGE BUTTERS COLLECTION)

FIGURE 102: Large circular mat worked in two colours (GEORGE BUTTERS COLLECTION)

The large circular mat has basic-braid outlines and whipped bars worked in cream. These form a pleasant contrast to the mushroom brown of the decorative braids and filling stitches. The mat is particularly rich in filling stitches. Their repetition in pattern sequence gives a sense of order and completeness to the design.

Two decorative crochet braids provide a lacy look for the outer edges. Both braids are held in place with a herringbone lacing. The fillings for the flower petals on the outer circle include ziggurat and arabesque. The decorations for the flower centres are backstitch wheel and stem-stitch wheel, alternating with petal weave. Leaf fillings are mainly variations of feather stitch worked over ladder bars and an impressive zigzag filling that widens and diminishes to fit the leaf shape.

The detail of the centre area of the mat shows the central flower and parts of the leaf and flower shapes in the border. The central flower has eight petals, all filled with divided wheat ear. The strung threads that form the woven filling give a lacy effect to the flower. A neatly worked backstitch wheel fills the flower centre. The inner circle of fancy braid is stitched with a matching thread directly into the narrow braid outlines. This large lace mat, which is a superior example of the art of Romanian point lace, would look attractive mounted under glass on a circular table.

The mat is approx. 59cm (23in) in diameter.

FIGURE 103: Detail of the central area of the large circular mat (GEORGE BUTTERS COLLECTION)

Further Reading

Articles on Romanian Point Lace

'Romanian Macramé Lace in the U.S.A.' by Jeanmarie Brucia, *Needle Arts*, December 2001

'Ioana Bodrojan's Romanian Point Lace' by Bart Elwell, *Piecework*, January/February 2001

Back copies of *Anna Burda* from the 1980s and 1990s

Back copies of *Stitchwork* from the 1930s

Books on Romanian point lace

Murariu, Sylvia. *Romanian Point Lace, a Course for Beginners*, self-published, 1996

Romanian Point Lace, a Course for Intermediates and Advanced, 1996

Tomida, Ecaterian. *Dantele din Puncte si Laseta*, published in Romanian by Edita Tehnica, Bucuresti, 1966

van den Kieboom, Ineke and Huijben, Anny. *The Technique of Tape Lace*, B T Batsford Ltd, 1994

Books on Needlepoint Lace

Hills, Ros and Gibson, Pat. *Needlelace Stitches, Classic and Contemporary*, B T Batsford Ltd, 1989

Lovesey, Nenia. *The Technique of Needlepoint Lace*, B T Batsford Ltd, 1980

Trivett, Lillie D. *The Technique of Branscombe Point Lace*, B T Batsford Ltd, 1991 (includes filling stitches)

Books on crochet

De Dillmont, Thérèse., ed. *Masterpieces of Irish Crochet Lace*, Dover Publications, Inc., New York, U.S. 1986 (includes instructions for the crochet leaf pattern)

Steams, Ann. *The Batsford Book of Crochet*, B. T. Batsford Ltd, 1981 (includes instructions for the basic braid)

Walters, James, and Cosh, Sylvia. *The Harmony Guide to Crochet Stitches*, Lyric Books Ltd. 1986

Brown, Nancy. *The Crocheters' Companion*, Interweave Press, 201 East Fourth St, Loveland, Colorado 80537, U.S. www.interweave.com

Embroidery and sewing techniques

Mary Thomas's Embroidery Book, first published by Hodder and Stoughton Ltd. 1936

Books on design

Gabor, Susan. *Treasury of Flower Designs*, Dover Publications, Inc. New York, U.S.

Lovesey, Nenia. *Creative Design in Needlepoint Lace*, B. T. Batsford Ltd, 1983 (butterfly patterns)

Mirow, Gregory. *A Treasury of Design for Artists and Craftsmen*, Dover Publications, Inc. New York, U.S.

The Schole-House for the Needle, produced from the book printed in 1632, now in the private collection of John and Elizabeth Mason. Published and produced for John and Elizabeth Mason by R.J.L Smith & Associates, Much Wenlock, Shropshire, England, 1998

STOCKISTS

SUPPLIERS IN THE U.K.

Threads, transparent blue film,
decoration starch, books:
Roseground Supplies
62 Chetwynd Road, Toton
Nottingham NG9 6FT.
tel/fax: 0115 972-0110
Mail order/email:
supplies@roseground.freeserve.co.uk
www.roseground.com

Turkish threads, Anchor crochet 20,
Coats Floretta crochet 10 & 20,
transparent blue film:
**Mary-Helen Tatting and Lacemaking
Supplies**
White Wheels, Aston Abbotts
Aylesbury, Bucks. HP22 4LU.
tel: 01296 681376
email:
mary@mary-helen.freeserve.co.uk

Anchor crochet 20, DMC Cordonnet
20, transparent blue film:
**Jo Firth Lacemaking and
Needlecraft Supplies**
58, Kent Crescent, Low Town,
Pudsey, West Yorkshire LS28 9EB.
tel/fax: 0113 257 4881
email: jo.firth@cwctv.net

Crochet threads:
Coats Crafts U.K.
PO Box 22, Lingfield House
Lingfield Point, McMullen Road
Darlington, Co. Durham DL1 1YQ.
Consumer Helpline: 01325 394237
email: consumer.ccuk@coats.com
www.coatscrafts.co.uk

Turkish threads, Candlelight Metallic:
Tatting and Design
47, Breedon Hill Road,
Derby, DE23 6TH.
tel/fax: 01332-383841
Mail order:
email: enquiry@tatting.co.uk
www.tattinganddesign.com

Threads, Books, Equipment:
The Lace Workshop
Unit 1 Blays, Churchfield Road
Chalfont St Peter, Bucks. SL9 9EW.
tel/fax: 0 1753 891161
email: sales@smplace.co.uk
www.users.zetnet.co.uk/smplace

Ready-worked lace braids and
finished lace articles from Romania:
Agent: George Butters
Woodend Farm, Hook Gate,
Market Drayton, Shropshire TF9 4QL.
tel: 01630 672230
(Allow a short time for items to be
sent from Romania.)

SUPPLIERS IN THE U.S.

Crochet threads, Manula & Flora size
20, DMC Cordonnet, crochet hooks,
blue contact paper, books:
Lacy Susan
4569 Rincon Place
Dumfries, VA 22026-1045
tel: (703) 580-1114
email: lacysusan5@aol.com
www.lacysusan.com

D.M.C. Cordonnet Spécial size 20,
blue contact paper, books:
Van Sciver Bobbin Lace

Holly Van Sciver
tel: (607) 277-0498
Shipments outside U.S. by airmail
email: vsblace@twcny.rr.com
www.vansciverbobbinlace.com

Books, Threads, Needlework
Supplies:
Jenny June Fancywork
249 Bear Creek Rd, Ruston, LA 71270
tel: 318-242-0017
email: Jenny@JennyJune.com
www.jennyjune.com

Threads, Romanian Lace patterns, kits:
D&E INTERTRADE Co.
1011 Marksworth Rd,
Baltimore, MD 21228
tel: 410-719-0062
email: d_e_ico@yahoo.com
http://members.tripod.com/victorian
art/index.htm

SUPPLIERS IN AUSTRALIA

Lacemaking materials, crochet
threads No 20 and 40, range of
crochet hooks
Crochet Australia
Ray and Vicki Moodie
PO Box 126, Wamuran Qld 4512
tel/fax: 07 54966826
email:info@crochetaustralia.com.au
Web:www.crochetaustralia.com.au

Threads, books, general lace items
Torchon House Lace Supplies,
Gaye Beswick,
c\o Post Office, Uraidla 5142,
South Australia
tel: 08 8390 1324.

FIGURE 104: Celtic set (Designed and made by Kathleen Waller. Photography by Bob Challinor)

FIGURE 105: Place mat set (Designed and made by Kathleen Waller. Photography by Bob Challinor)

INDEX